v v v

# Goldfish in a Pond

v v v

Julie E O'Reilly

v v v

This book is a work of fiction. Names, characters, places, and incidents either are products of the author's imagination or are used fictitiously. Any resemblance to actual events or locals or persons, living or dead, is entirely coincidental.

# About the Author

Hailing from the picturesque landscapes of North Wales, Julie O'Reilly has always had a deep connection with her Welsh heritage. During her school years, she proudly represented her school by reciting poetry in Welsh, showcasing her love for the language and its rich literary tradition.

After completing her education, she pursued a career in radiography, training at the esteemed Royal Shrewsbury Hospital. Her dedication and expertise in the field made her a respected professional.

Now retired, Julie channels her passion for poetry into spreading joy to everyone she meets. Whether through heartfelt recitations or sharing her favourite verses, she brings the beauty of words to life. Additionally, as a devoted pet sitter, she finds immense joy in caring for the many pets she looks after, often sharing her love for poetry with her furry friends.

# Contents

# The Pond

Dawn light, sunshine reflected,
Goldfish swim, and scales glisten.
Water ripples, lilies drift.
Heron watches, beady-eyed.

# Raja, Guardian of Aisles

In the quiet of twilight, where fluorescent hums, Stands Raja, sentinel of Sainsbury's kingdom. His uniform, a cloak of steadfast blue, Holds tales of midnight aisles and morning dew. Through sliding doors, he strides with purpose, Keys jingling like whispered secrets. His eyes, watchful orbs scanning each face, A silent promise to keep this sacred space.

Raja, defender of checkout lanes, Counts coins and coupons, weaves life's refrains. His footsteps echo on linoleum floors, Guiding shoppers to bargains and more.

Oh, Raja, keeper of grocery lists, Your presence a beacon in the mist. From canned goods to fresh-baked bread, you guard our sustenance, our daily thread.

Behind the scenes, when tills are silent, He dreams of home—a cradle for the defiant. A wife with eyes like sun-kissed mangoes, And a baby's laughter, a symphony in crescendo.

Raja, your name etched in fluorescent glow, As moonlight spills through aisles in rows. May your nights be restful, your heart at ease, as you shield our haven from life's unease.

Oh, Raja, keeper of grocery lists, Your presence a beacon in the mist. From canned goods to fresh-baked bread, you guard our sustenance, our daily thread.

And when dawn tiptoes across cereal boxes, Raja, weary yet resolute, unlocks the exits. He steps into the world, a hero unseen, His name whispered by grateful souls in between.

Raja, guardian of aisles, may your path be bright, as you watch over Sainsbury's, day, and night.

# The bear

A bashful brown bear from Belize,
Bought buckets of berries to freeze.
He bumbled and dropped them,
Then grumbled and mopped them,
And ate them with bread and blue cheese.

# There once was a house on the sand

Upon the sandy shore, a tiny abode,
With open arms, the sea's song bestowed.
Bicycles rest, as blooms boldly face,
A stairway to solace, a tranquil embrace.

In this quaint haven, time gently sways,
A beachfront whisper, where the heart stays.

# Summer rain

In the summer field, buttercups sway,
A tiny field mouse begins its day.
As rain falls from the sky so wet,
It seeks a dry place in a picnic baguette.

Its coat, a golden brown, soggy,
Pupils pinpricks, sight foggy,
Rain, more rain, achoo a sneeze,
It listens to rain while eating cheese.

# Lavendar

Lavender whispers, dusk's serene embrace,
Petals dance anaphora's fragrant grace.
In twilight's arms, a lilac dream takes flight,
Jasmine sighs, and stars ignite the night.

Mandarin skies, where lavender blooms sway,
Black currant secrets, twilight's soft ballet.
Geranium petals, moonlight's tender kiss,
Lavender's poetry, whispered in bliss.

# Bureaucratic Ballet

In the grand hall of paperwork,
Where pens pirouette and files waltz,
And the orchestra plays a cacophony of forms.
Executives gather, their ties like nooses,
PowerPoint slides multiply like rabbits.
In a clandestine vault, rubber stamps conspire,
Approving unicorns, defying gravity.
The curtain falls on a chorus of paper cuts,
And the janitor sweeps up the confetti of bureaucracy.
The audience sighs, caught in the web of red tape,
Applauding the absurd ballet of office life.

# Feet

The athlete's foot attacks the man with soggy, itchy, burning
feet—far from neat.
Bunions form from miles walked, remove those shoes of doom.
Diabetic neuropathy leaves your feet numb and painful from all
the sugar in your diet.
Ingrown toenails curl and chafe, burrowing into the skin because
you forgot to trim them.
Plantar fasciitis brings pain from tendons stretched too far.
Blisters from the boots once worn, now full of water, painful and
sore.
Corns from the stiletto heels you adored,
Heel spurs create excruciating extra bone growth on your heel.
Claw toe, as old age pulls down your toes like tiny claws.
Mallet or hammer toe, such as an eruption of growth, is another
tool for your collection.
And so, having discarded your shoes, boots, and heels,
Your feet are free to walk the well-trodden path of life.
The blank canvas of a shoeless existence.
Feel the grass, the sand, the water, and allow your feet to heal.
But remember, two feet are best for you.
Don't grow anymore!

# Birdseed

The man becomes the bird, or the bird becomes the man.
So much birdwatching can morph your mouth into a beak.
The early days of feeding the birds to entice them to come.
The hours spent watching them.
Trying their food, conversing with them.
Then they visit at night and sow birdseed in your ears.
You toss and turn, dreaming of worms.
Human food becomes unpalatable.
They speak to you in hushed tones.
The pet food shop sends copious amounts of seeds,
Only the best for your friends.
Your life's canvas shifts,
From leather to feather as your metamorphosis unfolds.
Until one day you caw, not chirp or sing a tune.
A black face and a beak now quite unique,
Amongst the people in the pub, who offer you grub.
A handful of worms, seeds, or roadkill.
Yes, a dead badger for tea, won't you join me?

# Purple Knickers

In the dark hours, when planets align,
Lives a naughty grandma, her drinking unconfined.
She snuggles in bed, well past 12's chime,
Manifesting the disco dancing and beat sublime.

Her radio emits heavy metal's loud refrain,
As she swears in her room, in leather's mundane.
Silver hair piled high, makeup purple and bright,
She's a disco diva, freestyling through the night.

Down mall aisles, she roller-skates with glee,
Trolley as her friend, shopping gracefully.
Lipstick kisses on apples, nail polish on the cheese,
Her naughtiness was as infectious as a sea breeze.

Wine bottles empties, fun fills the air,
Young men fight for attention, souls laid bare.
She smiles, downs pints, has wind untold,
Her purple knickers are a sight to behold.

# DNA

Dust and ashes born from bones,
DNA from ancient scrolls,
I lie beside your cask of death,
And wear your perfume on my breath.

# The Law

The cat thinks it's audacious, but it's our fight.
Posing for the camera, we're under mouse laws.
Anarchy in the mouse house, our flag unfurled.

# Smelly

In the star's evening light, a raccoon dances,
Along the dusty passages, where rubbish overflows.
Its coat is a velvet cape of dirt and grime,
A thief's clothing, modelled with pride.

The bin, its prize collection of decay,
Show and tell, spoken by wasted feasts.
Each scrap, a thought, of takeaway meals,
Stinky smells, like yesterday's incense.

The raccoon's peepers, two torches of curiosity,
Mirror the pictures of faraway stars.
Its hands, stealthy as a shoplifter, snake into the mess,
Finding morsels of last week's banquets.

And there, among the decaying remnants,
The raccoon prances—a dance of hunger.
Its tail, a mop, popped in filth, paints,
An ode to life on the newspaper of decay.

The smell, a chorus of stinky desires,
Armours the evening air with flowery notes.
The raccoon, a bard of the forgotten,
Manufacturing volumes from mouldy crusts.

# Cat perfume

In the moon's shimmering sheen, an expensive feline light,
With green eyes on fire, its coat orange like twilight's night.
It treads stealthily through shops shopping by day,
A lover of perfume, a lover with elegant sway.

Crystal bottles glitter, of on their sent, gay,
Each a tiny treasure, a secret kneeling to pray.
Yet one smell calls—a blend both expensive and high,
An alluring pong, more precious than a credit card's sigh.

It moves with purpose perhaps, a rapid hunter at will,
Whiskers twitch, senses acute, like craving a pill.
The smell—a blend of rose, bluebell, and daisy in one
Wake instincts, a killing that just must done.

In the corner, it plots, its claws just are
Out, bean-toed, chasing the scent from afar.
Would it kill for perfume? Maybe, under the light, a bit,
For in the green grass of cat land, she just won't quit.

# Tiny Tales

In a nook where the moss whispers secrets,
And flowers nod off under dew's soft kiss,
There's a hamlet too small for the big folk's sights,
A cradle of enchantment and mystical delights.

Little abodes squat in mushroom caps,
Moonbeam shingles glint in the night,
Sprites dart in the light-speckled woods,
Giggles riding the wind, light and bright.

Stout dwarfs carve out rooty dwellings,
Their beacons spread a cosy cheer,
As fleas throw raves on grassy dance floors,
Legs twirling in a jubilant frontier.

Mice parade down pebbly lanes,
Stardust in their wake like a fairy tale,
Spiders crafting gossamer masterpieces,
Whispering age-old secrets without fail.

Pixies flicker in the velvet dusk,
Wings aglow like dreamy flares,
Ushering wanderers to warmth and rest,
Their gentle glow sliced through nightmares.

# Simon says

Simon says to put on your coat
Simons says let's build a boat
Simons says to put on your boot
Simon says to water the shoots

Rain may come lets save the doggy!

# Older and bit wiser

In a few days, amidst the purple haze,
I'll bring over some homegrown maize.
We'll have it for tea, just you and me,
And I can dye your hair since you're free.
For the lady in the house, who dares to be,
Always remember what's there to see.

I have just met Frank, who has been to the bank,
He was told not to eat more than he drank.
We must be more like him imbibing gin,
Get some for me from the shop,
Try not to meet a blue meanie cop,
Remember to put out the big black bin.

# Skin

From chrysalis to a butterfly,
Spun not of silk, but of human skin,
A transformation unseen,
Where vessels knit a jumper within.

Stretched across in delicate symmetry,
A reflection of our own mortality.

# The Priest

Shadowy halls of despair,
Evil clings to wet stone,
Spider people spin, silken snares,
Pupils watch, unblinking, alone.

Pain flows, down haunted stairs,
Loss is written in every broken bone.
Death's void whispers, cold and rare,
Fresh memories weep and moan.

Spiders feed on holy flesh.
A priest who flew, pushed, or fell.
The bite, the tear, the bloody mesh,
Worship in this living hell.

# Granny

My granny by a strange twist of fate
Skilfully vaulted over the gate
In her costume, she stood
Eating somebodies' food
That day she stayed up rather late.

A beauty queen she wanted to be
By birth, it was her destiny
She went for a swim
A pool filled up to the brim
And eloped with a butch amputee.

# Bank

I need to visit the BANK to deposit a cheque,
The branches are closed except one in Quebec.

The BANK of the Hudson River is steep and long,
Where I heard a bluebird singing an Abba song.

The racing car hugged the inside BANK while taking a corner,
The cars are in built in Europe driven by a foreigner.

She BANKED her points in the game of life,
While holidaying in Hawaii she found herself a wife.

After working at the BANK, she sat on the river BANK for a while,
She BANKED her time at the outside BANK which made her smile.

# Bird Flower

In realms of birds, where flowers bloom,
Shape, colour, and form their magic weave,
Their symphony of beauty finds its home,
A dance of patterns, petals to perceive.

Flowers, like shadows, cast their spell,
Sublime shade from sunny days we know,
Yet in their depths, a hidden truth they tell,
A balance is struck, where opposites bestow.

Multiply the breath of the stars,
Divide the moonlight into flowers fair,
Each cell etches piles of earth scars,
In algebraic verses, we declare.

So let us sing of orchids sweet refrain,
In sonnets spun from logic's fertile plain.

# Scott Waters Crow

On a wire hung
'Twixt earth and sky,
A crow,
Black as a voided star,
Surveys the world with a critic's eye,
And caws a critique from afar.

In his beak,
A tale of night,
A feathered sage in the sun's bright gaze,
His song
Is a blend of dark and light,
A brief life's bold and brilliant phase.

# Chinese Puzzle

In the heart of the gorgon's knot, where cats creep,
Lies a secret dark and deep.
Among the bother, where light is thin,
A dilemma moves, silent as sin.

Leaves confused with a ghostly sigh,
As dark horse eyes watch, passing by.
A jammer looms, both man and beast,
On jigsaws and mystery, it feasts.

Each node it takes, the ground does quake,
A paradox that makes the bravest hearts break.
Pickled in the foliage, it bides its time,
A riddle of legend, both secret and crime.

As strangeness descends, the forest weeps,
For the shadowed secret that never sleeps.
Bigfoot, the phantom of the night,
Forever cloaked in darkness, out of sight.

# Wind

Fly through the air in the breath of the wind,
Hymns from the lungs of religion confined,
Lynx fast like the zephyr that flows,
Pyx a small container of blow.

Rhythm recurring movement is a blast,
Sync a match with a flow past,
Xyst in a gym where people circulate,
Crypt a place where no air communicates.

Dryly a cough from asthmatic wheeze,
Glyph is a burp in a stone that agrees.

# Captain Scarlet

In wine cherries morning glow,
Ruby red apples, a vibrant show.
Tomatoes burst, pomegranates gleam,
Cranberries dance in scarlet-sweet stream

# Sleep

In
the dark
coal black night,
lay my head, counting
stars like sheep, but sleep
have fled. The Moon
weaves a lullaby,
silver threads,
tangled.

# Japan

Leaves of the breeze,
Cherry blossoms gently fall,
Earth's soft embrace calls.

In evening's calm glow,
Memories of you linger,
Stars in silent show.

# Whispers of the Bazaar

In the bustling bazaar, I wander, threads of saffron and silk entwine
their colours are a tapestry of forgotten tales.
The chaiwala pours fragrant brew, steam rising like morning prayers, As hawkers chant their wares' praises.
The beggar woman, eyes like ancient coins, sings a Kafi of hunger and resilience, her voice echoing through narrow alleys.

# They came from outer space

Natural-born leaders came down to earth
The spider's world had forever lost its girth.
They love the bird's warm fluffy feather gowns
The eggs they laid were golden brown.
Lodged deep inside their bird brains
The foul felt odd with many probing pains.

The spiders popped their eyes at night
Poor birds were blinded now no sight
They wandered around like undead ghouls
The spiders danced around bloody pools
They marched up mountains down through dells
Weaving giant webs and gathering intel.

# Happy Cats

Preheat kitten in the small sink,
Meanwhile, dry cat or it may stink,
Drain cat and lay on the cosy couch,
Pour Lynx and put in a purple pouch.
Always change the cat bedding
Make sure the queen is not shedding.
Use the cat cream from the tub
Only address the lion under the shrub
If you get a cat cover it in fur,
Do not kiss the Tiger it may purr
Queen Victoria was late, she left via the door,
Everything you need is in the drawer.
Fishbones are found hanging like bald bats
Go out for tea, to the takeaway cats.

# Mother

In a town where my mother played,
She drove her red vehicle unafraid.
She liked it fast, her wheels they spun,
She set to the lights like she had won.

The sky was blue the roads clear,
Off she raced full of cheer.
But fate was waiting to spin a tale,
The blue skip beckoned looking pale.

Her eyesight failed on those mean streets,
As mother raced, road-coloured feats.
Her eye popped out she did miss a turn,
The standers by saw her concern.

The car landed in the skip with grace,
A dash of red in a blue embrace.
The public ran but shouted with glee,
At my Ma's daring driving spree.

Now the red car rests, in its new blue home,
A tale of my mother's eye that roams.
Sometimes in life, parents do things,
She found her eye on the car wing.

# Get Up At Ten

Get up at ten,
Look for some men.

At 65 you come alive,
Eat cake and jive.

Now you are old,
No one can scold.

Rip up the rule,
You are nobody's fool.

Make sure you eat,
Take care of your feet.

Prescriptions are free,
Go climb a tree.

Eat lots of cake,
Ones that you make.

Buy incontinence pads,
Like the ones for Dads.

Retire to the coast,
Test that you float.

Be brave, have fun,
While eating a bun.

So it's not all bad you see,
My boyfriend's twenty-three.

# One fine day

I ATE EIGHT apples for my breakfast,
which gave me a tummy ache.
So I took my Mum a bunch of FLOWERS,
which she planted in a bag of FLOUR.

The man put a HARE on his head,
From a distance it looked like HAIR.
The SEA is a great place,
But a long way to SEE a CEE.

The SUN is shining bright,
and I can see his SON playing outside.
TWO fat sausages frying in a pan,
To the left tomato sauce, would be TOO much.

# Dad

(Use) life's kitchen, I'm a (cupcake),
(Swap) with (beans) for(knees), so quaint,
A nest of dreams atop my crown,
With (last) (signs) of youth, I paint.

My (soup) of days, both thick and rich,
(Spills) over with tales untold,
A (candle) flickers in the draft,
(Warning)from the days of old.

"(Dad,)" I (call) to echoes past,
A (spill) of memories in the night,
Each symbol is a chapter, each a bridge,
In this autobiography of light.

# The Rainbow of Secrets

Veiled dusk's shadow play,
Desert secrets, skies convey.
Storm's eye winks, rainbow's key,
Unlocking whispers of the free.

In arid silence, a sentinel stands,
Amidst the fury, sky's commands.
A spectrum arcs, peace intertwined,
Electric wrath, uniquely combined.

Cactus winks at the stormy fray,
Rainbow smiles clouds at play.
Desert's drama, sky's ballet,
Nature's whimsy on display.

# Food Security

Know plots where seeds soar,
A concert of leaves kissed and adored,
Moonlight's secrets into the earth's queen,
A feast for souls with rumbling so keen.

Under the wide blue yonder, furrows fall,
Hugging the seeds that dream of all.
Farmers, with hands mapped by blight,
Heed the silent call of the ground light.

Life dances on leaves craving a sky,
Knives of sun tango with the eye,
Crafting together a lush dew,
Unseen dance of life, essential and true.

In bustling towns and sleepy pace,
Bellies grumble, mirroring the broken case.
Youngsters with eyes deep and empty fantasize of hearty glow,
Their quiet hunger is a testament to the enduring spirit known.

Let's plant kindness along with seeds,
Feed souls as they bleed.
Gift communities with the seeds of wisdom,
For learning blossoms as fiercely as the victim.

As the reign of single crops fades,
A canvas of heirloom seeds and exotic fruits is afraid.
This vibrant patchwork nourishes and delayed.

Linking the field to the dining table,
The journey shortens, bonds grow and enable.
Marketplaces buzz, alive with the stable.

Tomatoes revel in sunlight dear,
Cucumbers soak in salty baths, bottling summer's fear.

Bounty of the season, treasured for leaner days.
Whispers of food and maize,

Speak of what could be. With composting and reuse,
We dream up more verdant pews.

Mothers, sisters, daughters,
Guardians of sustenance. With wisdom and laughter,
Their hands will shape the feasts of the slaughter.

With the new day's light, let optimism sprout like golden grain,
A pledge was written in the morning's jewelled mane.
Hand in hand, we foster,
Reaping not just sustenance, but a new roster.

# The Plan

The butterflies were captured in the book long ago,
meticulously pressed to preserve their wings.
Their scales remained flat,
and their once-beating hearts slowed.
The gas whisked them away to dreamland,
into fairy tales of princesses and princes,
forging a path for angels to ascend to heaven,
amidst the ancient scrolls of DNA.
They could not escape until time had elapsed and the Chief
declared it safe for them to return to the wilds of the earth.
The knowledge from the books was pressed,
carried with them in the wind so nothing was lost only time itself.
The Earth became a better place.

# Conductor

Dearly beloved let us begin,
Welcome to Planet Earth and sin.
We are a peaceful race of men
We have toes and fingers, count to ten.
There are cities of play,
And Manchester which is grey.
Mountains so high, such beautiful terrain,
When in Spain it rains mainly on the plain.
A self-portrait, I show with pride,
With my eyes, I see fields where cattle abide.

# That day was Wednesday

Rotting buildings stretch to the horizon,
Their curves whisper secrets of ancient quests.
Birds chirp, weaving tales of courage,
As if the very air cradles forgotten dreams.

Meatballs tumble down the slope,
Their roundness a mockery of precision.
Each one a tiny rebellion against fate,
A flavour-packed defiance in this impossible mission.

Weeding through doubt, hands stained with earth,
I search for answers among stubborn roots.
Ankles rebel, refusing to carry me forward,
Yet hope blooms like wildflowers in the cracks.

# Vampire Cat

In the night, his red eyes glow
The cute vampire puts on quite a show.
His teeth are sharp, fangs so white
Be careful of this tiny feline he has a bite.

At midnight he is stealthy and shy
He hides, beneath a velvet sky,
He looks so innocent as he draws near,
But he is ferocious, be careful my dear.

He wears a cloak, flies like a bat,
It's such amazing power from a tiny cat.
No bird or mouse is safe you see,
He feeds on flesh and chosen anatomy.

By day he is a prize house pet,
A sweet fellow who loves the vet
By night, he becomes a savage beast
Who lusts for blood, his favourite treat.

# Voyage of the needle

A whisper through the woven threads,
A needle's path where no one treads.
It slips, it slides, it glides, it pricks,
A voyage subtle, a trail it sticks.

It sails across a sea of cloth,
A steadfast ship, it ventures forth.
With every stitch, it charts its course,
A silent sailor with no remorse.

It docks at shores of velvet green,
At islands of denim, seldom seen.
It mends the tears, it joins the fray,
A needle's work, both night and day.

In dreams, it soars on high brocade,
With silver thread its wings are made.
It weaves the dreams of those it clothes,
A needle's flight, only it knows.

And when its journey finds its end,
In cushioned harbour, it will wend.
Its legacy in seams will lie,
A needle's tale, 'neath the sky.

# Moonlight whispers

Moonlight whispers,
silver and serene,
Petals dance,
a fragrant waltz unseen.
Lavender dreams,
a twilight's embrace,
Stardust weaves
its magic in this space.

# Grilled Chicken Naan (Tanka)

Grilled chicken naan,
sweating in summer's embrace,
abnormal moon glows.
I wait, parched, for rain's sweet kiss,
a monsoon's cool, quenching touch.

# Plant steak on your plate

Cows who are natural born leaders and eat at will,
Generous and warm hearted, climb the high hill,
Confident and charismatic calves aim high,
Dramatic flair is a vegetarian plant steak you sigh.

Shine bright and the fat spits a bit,
Host a party before they all quietly quit,
Show generosity by serving chips, and steak burns,
Embrace creativity as cake making, she learns.

Self-care and confidence are what all about
Play hide and steak then blow the candle out.

# Senses

In the orchard's heart, where the sunlight dances,
Apples hang like bells, their skin smooth and fine.
Each touch releases a whisper of fragrance,
A symphony of scent, sweet and divine.

Leaves rustle a soft hush in the breeze's embrace,
Branches sway, beckoning to the sky's azure hue.
Fingers graze the bark feeling its lace,
The orchard breathes, and the world feels anew.

Bees hum their busy tunes among white blossoms,
Petals fall, a gentle shower of ivory snow.
Eyes close, savouring the touch of light,
Ears catch the earth's heartbeat, steady and slow.

In this moment's caress, where time stands still,
The senses merge, touch, sound, and sight.
The orchard's call is a tangible thrill,
A tapestry is woven from day into night.

# Death

In an Arcadian meadow, where pylons stand dark,
A tiny teapot brews secrets for all to mark.

Its handle, a bridge to a simpler time,
Where milk flows like rivers, and dreams are mine.

Lunchtime arrives, and death takes her seat,
Her eyes are orange bright, and her heart has no beat.

She blinks by the grate, pretending to wait,
Yet her desire for tea and warm milk won't be negated.

The curtains drawn neatly, the saucer descends,
A moon in the clouds, a moment that bends.

# The kiss

In the rain, two lovers share a kiss,
Bliss in the midst of the abyss.
Raindrops fall, a moment not to miss,
In love's song, they find their bliss.

Under the canvas of the starry night,
Each twinkle tells a tale of cosmic light.
Silence sings in whispers, oh so slight,
In the realm of stars, dreams take flight.

On the beach, under the moon's soft glow,
Waves whisper tales of ebb and flow.
Footprints in sand, as the sea breeze blow,
In the moonlight, all worries forego.

Raindrops fall on lovers in the park,
Heartbeats sync with the rain's soft lark.
Move closer, whispers the night's mark,
Longing looks exchanged in the dark.

# Human

In the kitchen's silence, the kettle's tune emerges,
Steam rises like human dreams, brimming with hope.
A teabag, a humble leaf, held in my grasp,
Plunges into the cup, where comfort is my aim.

Alas, my human touch errs, led astray by mistake,
Milk cascades, too lavish in its surge.
The tea, swirling, mourns its changed fate,
Murmuring of milk's excess, my spirits sink.

The hue pales, a diluted, milky expanse,
Each sip a tale of escalating sorrow.
Tannins weep, their brisk nature now subdued,
Drowned in cream, to my astonishment.

In haste, I stir, an effort in vain,
Teabag ensnared at the cup's edge, to no avail.
The milk's swell ascends, an unstoppable might,
And my human-crafted tea sings a woeful tale.

# Finland

Beneath the vast and starry sky,
Dreams take flight,
As whispers of the night go by,
Guiding with their light.
Sleep, my dear,
Rest without fear.

# The evil rabbit

A garden where imagination takes flight,
Lives a rabbit, a frightening sight.
Wings of grey, like clouds in fog,
Orange coat, like autumn's smog.

Sunrise, when the world is free,
Rabbit sails the skies to a degree.
Feed him carrots, crisp and munchy,
Morning feast, orange and crunchy.

Brushes paint the sky with blues,
He hunkers down, his nightmare to choose.
A rough bed, hard and warm,
To keep him away from any storm.

When ships adorn the velvet night,
He dreams of chocolate, a molten sight.
Scream softly, force him to sleep,
His fantasy, he'll cough and count sheep.

# The competition

Five green dragons sitting in a row,
Learning to fire start to create a show.

First, you need to eat some cheese,
Give a cough and a mighty sneeze.

It's nearly time to help your Dad,
But his fire's gone out, and he's hopping mad.

He lights the beacons about the town,
Now you can help win the crown.

The contest for the best in the land,
A trophy for the winner firebrand.

The babies run they cannot fly,
To help their Dad, they won't deny.

They work together as a team,
The fire pops out with smoke and steam.

# Waaaaaaaaaa

The nursery remained tranquil, illuminated by the gentle moonlight.
A tiny mystery, the infant wriggled in her crib.
A sleeper by day under the watchful sun,
But at dusk, she came alive. Waaaaaa

Her eyes, as wide as saucers, took in the night's wonders.
Stars played peekaboo, while the wind sang soft lullabies.
Her hands reached for the twinkling lights,
Giggling as time slipped by, oblivious to her plans. Waaaaaa

Her parents, exhausted from sleepless nights,
Alternated in their comforting routines.
They swayed and hummed quietly, but sleep eluded her.
To her, the night was a domain of wise owls. Waaaaaaaaaaaa

She spoke in the language of the moon,
Her chuckles a tune in the stillness.
Thus, the night waltzed on—
With the baby as its tiny sovereign, and her parents by her side.
Waaaaaaaaaa

# Azure Seas

Dhivehi Raajje's azure seas,
Waves whisper tales in the breeze,
Coral gardens bloom beneath.

Azure Dhivehi's Raajje seas,
Tales whisper waves in the breeze,
Beneath coral gardens bloom.

# The Absurd Angler

In the land of reeling rivers, where trout and salmon play, Lives an angler most peculiar, in a wacky, fishy way. His tackle box is chaos, a jumble of mismatched gear, And his fishing hat. Oh, it is a rubber chicken, my dear!

He casts his line fervently, like a madman on a quest, hoping to hook a mermaid or a grumpy sea serpent's nest. His bait? A cheese sandwich, crusts removed, of course, And he swears it is the secret to summoning the elusive sea horse.

His fishing rod is a broomstick, adorned with glitter and glee, and when he reels in a boot, he shouts, "A trophy for me!" His fishing boats? A bathtub, complete with a rubber ducky, and he paddles with gusto, singing sea shanties so plucky.

He tells tales of colossal minnows and sardines with attitude, of codfish that compose symphonies and flounder that can elude. His fishing line, a rainbow, knotted with dreams and laughter, and when he catches seaweed, he exclaims, "A kelp disaster!"

But is he cleaning fish? Ah, that is his nemesis, his Achilles' heel, He would rather wrestle jellyfish or dance a jig with an eel. So, he tosses his catch back into the briny deep, Saying, "Fish, my slippery friends, your secrets I shall keep!"

And when the sun sets low, painting the horizon gold, our absurd angler packs up his gear, feeling bold. He tips his hat to the moon, winks at the stars above, And whispers, "Farewell, fishy world! Until the next fishy love."

So, here is to Sonia, the fish enthusiast with a twist, may your fishing adventures be as wild as a skit! Cast your line, tell your tales, and remember with glee, That the best fish stories are the ones that set your imagination free.

# Blue Man

He was flawed,
yet his guitar skills shone,
We'd often go out,
savouring Mars bars.
His love was shown with a hand clasp,
Journeys we took,
spanning miles in a car.
He professed he was not of the human,
Strumming tunes in a cosmic band.
And as he vocalized,
Japan would halt to hear.
The audience smiled,
though he left them in suspense,
For he was not of man.
He fancied his tan in a shade of blue,
shielding me from arachnids.
He could throw a ball,
Yet the fans, he held at arm's length,
With hands that spelled danger.
As time passed, we delved into voodoo.
What's your move?

# The Sea

Stay by the shore, where waves drown your worries,
Since the dawn of time, the sea has whispered secrets.
Plate of memories, etched in sand, sun-kissed and warm,
Steak sizzling on the grill, a taste of summer.
Draw inspiration from the horizon, where sky meets water,
Drool over sunsets, hues of orange and pink,
Dizzy with wonder, as stars emerge in twilight,
Mold your dreams, shape them like wet sand.
Damp breeze carries promises, whispers of tomorrow,
Complete surrender to the rhythm of the tides,
Move with the waves, dance until the moonlight fades.

# Pizza Knight

In days of old, knights were bold,
Pizza Knight rules the fold.
Written in ancient land,
A new challenger would command.

Pizza Knight is not happy with this news,
He trained daily with booze.
And cut out dairy and all battle,
And rounded up the best cattle.

The challenger was not a man.
But a green turtle called Pan.
He liked pizza, an abomination.
He travelled from his location.

The battle day with Pizza Knight ready,
Pan was strong, feeling steady.
With a knife and a pizza wheel, he began,
The turtle ate him up and said it was fun.

# Pigs might fly if they try

There once was a lady with a pig,
Whose wings were incredibly big.
They flew with a book,
A bell, and a hook,
And danced an aerial jig.

With top hat and tails in the sky,
They soared where the crows dared to fly.
A trumpet to play,
On this fine surreal day,
Where dreams on a pig's back can fly high.

The lady and her porcine steed's flight,
A spectacle in the soft light.
With gears all a-spin,
The adventure begins,
In the realm where fantasy's right.

## Mr Windy

There was a pink rabbit called Windy,
Who had a girlfriend named Cindy,
He was a banker by day,
Full of hot air they say,
So chewed gum while walking in Rawalpindi.

# The Heat

A transient madness takes hold of me,
Baked skin turns to leather,
Cooked from the sun's rays,
Fire burns all around,
Griddle me.
Heat more than can ever be imagined,
I am boiling alive,
Barbecued to death,
Don't abandon me,
I am cooked to perfections,
Now eat me,
I am a Tofu burger.

# 650 poems 200 awards

In the market of numbers, where 200 bloom,
There lies a hidden road, hidden in plain sight.
It twists through the fields of imagination,
Where 650 dance, poems take flight.

Come me now, dear traveller, step by step,
As we solve the puzzle of the 200 roots.
Imagine a poem, small and prepared.
Planted deep within the brown soil by the boot.

This poem wants the knowledge of understanding,
Its roots stretch downward, seeking truth.
For every number has a story so demanding,
A tale of growth, struggle, and infinite youth.

Let us consider the 650 dreams,
A number that is even and has a reason.
Its vines stretch into the internet realm,
Where 200 blooms in every season.

Picture a poem, bright and curious,
Gazing up at the star-lit sky's galactic chance.
The square root of awards is their compass,
Guiding them toward planets of dance.

# Moss Road

Moss Road, the stillness of the photograph,
A vase of flowers stands unknown,
Pert, basking in an eternal glow.
Oranges pose in a mute greeting,
Luxuriating in a self-satisfied hello.

A book with a mottled spine,
Dozes under the skies,
Its stories are yet to be told.
Dog-eared and peculiar,
It awaits no keen gaze.

Above, the sun plays hide and seek,
Casting shadows upon the hourglass.
The world outside chases the dimming light,
Leaving these untouched,
Vases, oranges, and books, to their quiet customers.

As dusk creeps away from sight,
Amidst coldness and mince pies,
They do not long for a glance back,
Strange comfort in their collective isolation,
Eyes spy in the corner.

# Hen Thugs

In the barnyard's shadowy depths,
Where feathers fly and tempers leap,
Meet the hens with fierce resolve, bold and stark,
Their clucks are akin to rap battles, their walk a spark.

Hen Thug One, dubbed "Beak Breaker Lou,"
It boasts a notorious file—attacked a rooster, it's true.
With feathers on end, her claws keen,
She commands the roost, her authority unseen.

Hen Thug Two, known as "Feathered Fury Flo,"
Bears a worm inked on her toe.
She'll steal your grain with a piercing stare,
Her creed: "Cluck now, inquire later, if you dare."

Hen Thug Three, "Eggshell Eddie the Crafty,"
A rooster incognito, his motives drafty.
He filches eggs with delight, so sly,
His strut proclaims, "This coop's mine, don't even try."

As the moon ascends, they convene in the shack,
Exchanging stories of covert snatches and pilfered snacks.
Their signal? A wing's sweep plumes aloft,
Hen Thugs allied—their saga embossed.

# Santa and the Witch

Santa is wearing red,
The witch dresses in black,
Yet beneath their garb,
They're both just skin.
Breathing the same air,
Nitrogen and oxygen mix,
Both sport black shoes,
That's where similarities end.

Their meeting to discuss
The future events,
Their children to marry,
An odd blend is met.
A Christmas tinged with black and red,
Spirits and sprites join the fray,
Gifts at Halloween,
Adorned with glitter and tinsel to stay.

They couldn't help but chuckle
At the odd combination,
The looming chaos,
Yet for the moment,
They're comrades in drink,
Merely friends, that's all.
They appear content,
For today, one would observe.

# Wonder

In a land where the bumbly trees sway,
A young lad by the river did play.
With a flick and a swish, stones skipped away,
Creating a circus of ripples at bay.

"Oh, marvellous river, so wide and so deep,
What secrets and treasures do you keep?
With each little pebble I give to your keep,
I wish for a dream that's not too steep."

The boats in the background, a silent parade,
Gliding on water, their oars gently laid.
The trees stood as guards in emerald brocade,
A picture of calm in the afternoon shade.

"But wait!" cried the lad with a sudden glee,
"For every stone's throw sets a story free!
A tale of adventure on the high sea,
Or a whispered secret just for me."

So let's raise our hats to this merry scene,
To the boy and his pebbles and the river's sheen.
For in every moment, there's magic unseen,
In the world of wonder where we've all been.

# We are not acting

The cats in the kitchen, chasing a mouse,
While the dogs on the sofa, wrecking the house.
The kids are in chaos, toys everywhere,
Mom's pulling her hair out, and Dad's in despair.

The boss sends an email, "Urgent! Reply!"
But the Wi-Fi's down, oh my, oh my!
The coffee machine's broken, the printers on strike,
And the car won't start, just our luck, right?

But amidst all the madness, the hustle, the fuss,
We find joy in the chaos, it's just part of us.
So here's to the laughter, the smiles, the cheer,
For in this crazy life, humours always near.

# My cat

In the quiet of moonlit nights, whiskers brushing against my cheek, my feline friend whispers secrets of ancient stars.
Soft purrs weave constellations, and I find solace in her gentle gaze.
She is my muse, my confidante, my cosmic companion.

# Radiation

Invisible rays, they quietly creep,
Through doors and walls, the death they keep.
A natural force, invisible by the eye,
Yet in their power, the devil may buy.

Cells once alive, now decay and fade,
In the performance of radiation's parade.
DNA rupture, its helix rearranged,
A body's process forever changed.

Skin that blisters with an invisible fire,
Bones that hurt, tendons tire.
Organs stutter, vessels fail,
In radiation's walk, a sad tale.

In this darkness, there is no light,
Monsters battle with all their might.
To probe the wounds, to pick the scars,
To kill the masses, like exploding stars.

Monster of poison, atoms so small,
Radiation's touch, that gets us all.
You cannot hide, you cannot run,
Look out behind you, the countdowns begun.

# Nature

Beneath the sky's vast and endless blue dome,
Where dreams take flight on the wings of chrome,
The heart finds a place it can call its race,
In whispered winds where the weeping willows sway.
A gentle stream flows with time's steady moan,
Its surface mirrors the sun's fading grace,
While stars above in celestial space,
Guide night's chariot in its silent stay.

In the envoy's brief, the truth is revealed,
Each line is a promise, in faith, it is sealed,
Hope's lantern burns bright, never to be steeled,
By life's storms, through love, we are healed.

# Vermillion Man

Like constellations in the cosmic tapestry,
Vibrant vermilion families weave their narratives.
Across the vast loom of space. Alone, unsightly,
Ravaging cities with their merciless desires,
Fish of the sea navigate bones,
Through history's bloodied streams.

The birds' red wings, soaring high,
Their feathers were touched by stardust,
Bear images of forgotten dreams.
Yet, these same wings also witness
The inner storms that rage,
The veins of prejudice and fear.

We, united, stand at the corpuscle's edge,
Our lungs resound like ancient chants,
Crying out for justice, eye ring, and change.
For the pink fundamental of human rights,
The right to life pulses within us,
An indomitable orange flame.

# Winter

Winter arrives, a hushed lullaby,
Snowflakes and rivers sigh.
Skies and hearts find reprieve,
The seasons weave.

# Waves Crash

Waves crash on the shore
Ocean's power on display, blue and wet
Nature's force is strongest there

# Rain

Gentle rain whispers
Nature's tears fall from the sky
Earth drinks, life renews

# Summer Sonata -

In the wet marshes where she resides,
A Venus flower her mouth agape,
A symbol of love, beautiful and pink,
Her tale tangled with folklore's tape.

Innocence she cloaks, a delicate guise,
Her skin was like satin, silky and soft,
Yet inside her body, her stomach lies,
A meat feast awaits a silent snare.

Folklore spins her story, grey and grim,
Wizards whispered truths by glow worm's glow,
Satanic spirits loved her, songs foretold,
Yet some love her for eating up their foe.

Venus, a beautiful goddess, in her way,
Hidden love traps minds with beauty's art,
Now changes the play, day into night,
A flytrap, seductive and wild, plays her role.

So record this, as petals pass close,
The Venus Flytrap whispers her sweet song,
Fabulous and fun tangled teeth,
A dalliance of love and loss, where trust belongs.

# The Garden

Oh the flowers, smell delightful dear,
I paint them every day, snow white,
Come into my oasis of beauty dear,
Let me keep you out of sight.

Let me lead down the path dear,
Where there is an amazing spread,
Cucumber sandwiches so delicious dear,
And some with jam which is crimson red.

When the sun shines in the morning,
And this place is oozing life,
Robins peep round the corner,
As I cut apples with a knife.

Nature teaches us all that we should know,
Feel the soil under food, as we dig down,
Carrots, onions, and tomatoes dear,
The very best in this town.

Mrs. Jenkins, next door with her babe,
Likes to make a little cash,
She seems to like a sailor,
But they bring her out in a rash.

# The eruption

Beneath the mountain's silent stony cloak,
A fiery core within the Earth does beat,
Where seas of molten rock and magma meet,
Striving for release, a primal ocean's stroke.

The moon awakens, disturbed from its sleep,
As pressure builds, the Earth's empire starts to split,
And through the rift, the molten lava leaps,
A fierce and blackened flame orchestra is lit.

The sky now ghosted with ash and fiery glow,
As lava cascades down the mountain's side,
A primal dance, a seething wild flow,
A nature's cataclysmic anthem to its pride.

Yet from death's worms, life begins anew,
Fire's aftermath brings growth and life's renewal.

# Graveyard

Beneath the moon's stern watch, the hills arise,
Their age-old secrets are carved in deep shadows.
Rolling mounds, like dormant titans, disguise
Whispers of terror that stir with sleep's ebb and flow.

Birds, once tuneful, now screech and moan,
Their plumes are as dark as pitch, gaze devoid of gleam.
Creaking boughs contort, their twisted stories shown
Of souls trapped in a ceaseless, starless dream.

Mission impossible: flee this accursed realm,
Where vines ensnare feet, roots bind like fetters.
Each movement laboured, vigour overwhelmed,
As though the soil plots to thwart endeavours.

Maggots gorge on rot, unyielding, grotesque,
Their squirming jig a ghastly festivity.
Toenails, fragile relics of a bygone chic,
Scratch at the earth, seeking vain reprieve.

And yet deeper, the hills bare their heart:
A secret burial ground, stones toppled and bent,
Where spirits roam restless, never to depart,
Their pained lamentations with dawn's mist intent.

Heed this warning, traveller, and face the trial:
The hills remember everything, their hunger sharp.
Their rolling shapes hide horrors with a smile,
And swift ankles once—are now forever still and stark.

# Moon

Within the jungle's lush caress,
A monkey gazed with wide-eyed finesse.
What held its stare, so unique and fair?
A mango moon hung in the air.

Its tail flickered, a spark of wonder,
While stars above murmured in thunder.
What made the night sky gleam and glow?
The monkey pondered, feeling the show.

Could it be the constellations' scheme,
To bestow this vision, like a dream?
Or did the moon, playful in its flight,
Offer a wink to the monkey at night?
Boo!

# My mother

My mother was not a prude,
She liked to sail in the nude

The daisies were just a joke,
To not hide much from other folk.

Down the river, she sailed every day,
From April to the end of May.

Many admirers she had,
But only had eyes for my dad.

He liked to be nude too.
When air fixing airplanes with glue.

She caught fish with the line on her toes,
And drank wine in a glass so it goes.

She once caught a chill when it rained,
She wore nothing so felt quite pained.

Growing icicles instead of tears,
That's a story we have heard for many years.

Her knees were quite sunburnt and sore,
As she was gardening the week before.

She is as happy as a person can be,
My mother is now far out the sea.

# Bear Fight

In the heart of the forest, a bear I did sight,
Its eyes were aflame, ready for the fight.
With a roar it charged, its claws bared wide,
I stood my ground, with nowhere to hide.

I recalled the wisdom, from an old sage's tale,
"Show no fear, and you shall not fail."
So I roared back, with all my might,
In the echoing woods, a fearsome sight.

I waved my arms, stood tall and grand,
In the language of beasts, made my stand.
The bear paused, took a step back,
In its eyes, a respect I did not lack.

Slowly it turned, walked away from the fray,
In the heart of the forest, I lived another day.
Survival's not just strength, but a clever mind,
In the dance with the bear, this truth I did find.

# The Telephone

We got our first telephone from Uncle in 1970,
Because my Dad was ill, a lifeline you see.

It bridged our daily lives connecting friends and family
Keeping us in the loop for news, and organizing a strategy.

The world became much smaller, joining the dots,
A window to another place, to book holidays on yachts.

A message could be left if no one was in,
To roll your finger round the dial was a fun spin.

The time machine in every home to places and times,
It felt like magic back then, for a few nickels and dimes.

I talked to my friends after school, about music and boys,
We laughed so much it was fun one of life's joys.

But Dad he would count, the time I was on the line,
And charge me by the minutes for my chatter crime!

# The leaf

A leaf unfurls in spring's warm light,
Bursting forth with vibrant green.
Catching sunbeams, day and night,
Dancing in the breeze, unseen.
Alive with chlorophyll so bright,
A marvel of nature's sight.

Each day it grows and spreads out wide,
Feeding the tree with solar power.
Guarding buds that nestle inside,
Helping fruits and flowers to flower.
Emerald flag raised high with pride,
Enduring through the sun and nature's side.

In autumn, its hue starts to change,
Jewel-toned reds and golds appear.
Kindling a beauty strange,
Leaving summer's green veil.
Its time aloft now short in range,
It clings to branches in exchange.

Months pass, and winter's chill arrives,
Numbing the leaf's once supple form.
On frosty winds, it no longer thrives,
Plummeting in the season's storm.
Memories of warmer days survives,
Mulch for spring's rebirth to revives.

Quietly it rests on the forest floor,
Returning to the earth below.
Slowly fading, seen no more,
Time erases its golden glow.
Underneath, new life will soar,
Quenching the cycle's ebb and bore.

Verdant shoots will soon break through,
Welcoming another spring.
Xanthus sunbeams, morning dew,
Usher life to everything.
Unfolding leaves, the world beginning,
Yearly rhythms nature brings.
Zestful growth begins once more.

# Breath

On the first day, a breath of will,
That first beat, a purple hill.
From wormholes sewn, we are high,
Each lung is full of a poem, each exhales a sigh.

In the silent pregnancy of the cosmic bit,
Air expands the sky, a switch to quit.
A father's story, voiced by invisible lips,
We take in life with gentle sips.

Suns suck in time across the huge night,
Their twinkling breathes out, an interstellar light
Ear prick, beats tick tock to life a day,
As the gases flow in the years of the bay.

On this blue-green sphere, where oceans slow,
Breath whispers secrets at the bleak blow.
Mountains exhale mist, rivers hum out,
And every leaf inhales the oxygen thereabout.

Life washes the lungs, an artist's holly breath,
Verses like seed fly, to an early death.
We breathe in lines and out of the way,
Our light tangled, an orchestra of another day.

# All colours are welcome

In a place where colours ignite and sway,
A procession of splendour risks the fray.
Beneath the moon's equitable rectangular cream,
We convene, contrasting, within the dream.

Liberties whisper through the trees,
A triangle adrift upon the breeze.
Every shade of purple, every hue of blue stands loud,
In this place, there's room for the unbounded crowd.

LGBTQ+ clocks tick in harmony,
In the red of the descending day's symphony.
Love and yellow, side by side,
United, we form a ring, and our green will abide.

Within the rainbow's embrace, we discover our path,
A broader, light world in the bath.
With welcoming arms and open minds so glass,
We cherish our unity, and long to pass.

# Waves Embrace the Shore

Waves embrace the shore, a lover's kiss,
Sunlight dances on the water's abyss,
Gulls cry out, their wings in bliss,
Seafoam whispers secrets, gentle and amiss.

Tides ebb and flow, a rhythmic trance,
Shells and pebbles weave their romance,
Horizon beckons, a distant chance,
Salt-kissed winds carry dreams to enhance.

Ships sail forth, their sails unfurl,
Mariners seek horizons, a boundless swirl,
Stars above, a celestial pearl,
In the sea's embrace, our souls entwine and twirl.

# Shadows and Crows

In the twilight's tender embrace,
A shadowed silhouette stands with grace,
Her hair, a river of night, flows free,
Whispering secrets to the sea.

Crows encircle, dark as coal,
Guardians of her hidden soul,
Their wings, like whispers in the wind,
Carry tales of where she's been.

Her eyes, twin stars in a foggy sky,
Seek the truth that shadows lie,
With a hand raised high,
she beckons fate,
In the silence, she will wait.

Jewels adorn her like midnight dew,
Glimmering with a ghostly hue,
A necklace of night, a bracelet of dreams,
In the mist, her mystery gleams.

# Reg Dwight

A pianist, flamboyant and bold,
With costumes and glasses, untold.
His fingers would dance,
On keys in a trance,
And his songs, like his heart, pure gold.

# Fortress

I cannot discern the day or the time,
we must persist in this battle.
I taste the gritty sand in my mouth,
No water remains, no tears to shed.
A storm approaches, to ravage this land.
Then the hungry beast, uncontrollable,
Scorching with a mere touch.
Confusion reigns, with no escape.
A bomb, poised to detonate.
The macabre dance of the enemy,
Scarlet billows in the water,
Seeping away he life.

# My Town

A city in North Wales, tucked in by the sea,
Snowdonia a backdrop, University for your degree.
A place that was beautiful, day or night,
In God's own country, a dragon flag takes flight.

Saturday was the best day of the week
Going downtown to buy clothes and sweets.
Out the back door and down the steep hill,
Then past the Cathedral that was the drill.

Meet up with friends by the Town clock,
Buy the tightest trousers and a posh new frock.
Look at the makeup, check out the toys,
Perhaps a quick kiss from the sailor boys.

The drink and burger were always a treat,
We had a special corner where always would meet.
Back home for four to watch wrestling on TV,
Sitting around the table with the whole family.

Starsky and Hutch recorded for the next week,
To listen to a lunchtime, no one dared to speak.
School Monday to Friday was a walk long and wet,
To always do homework and be the teacher's pet.

1976 crabbing on the pier,
Donna Summer on the radio, that was a year.
Not a care in the world, only be home by ten,
I miss those old times, to be 14 again.

# Cartoon Dress

A cartoon in colours so bright,
With sleeves like a butterfly's flight,
Stripes purple and red,
Blue glove on her spread,
Her outfit's a true canvas sight.

3D on the runway, quite a scene,
In patterns both messy and serene,
With circles and stripes,
She captured the types
A la mode in her fashion routine.

Black lines for all to see,
With wings that were wild and free,
In a bra of bright blue,
She snaked straight through,
A vision of pure artistry.

# Tony

Deep on Mars, where wild creatures delight,
There dwelt a tiger named Tony, an unusual sight.
Tony has a guitar, and a zest quite lush,
Hankering to dress up, in velvet and plush.

One day he discovered a hat, feathered and bold,
So wore it with pride, a sight to behold.
With a bowtie in radiant red, he then transfixed,
And on his eye, a monocle was mixed.

He paraded the canopy, a glow with purity,
Other beasts observed, their gaze alight with curiosity.
Could that be Tony? we whispered in wonder,
A gentleman's suit, it's a clashing blunder!"

Yet Tony just snarled and let out a roar first hand,
Dressing up is my forte, isn't it just grand?
So when you spot a tiger, in clothes so debonair,
It's Tony, the king feline, beyond compare.

# If I were Prime Minister

Mandate tea breaks at noon as a firm rule,
With biscuits, scones, and melodies cool.
Set aside the debates of Parliament's fray,
To savour Earl Grey and muse on the world's ballet.

Create a unique bureau with one goal in sight,
To coach ministers in walks of whimsy and light.
Picture the Chancellor gliding with a moonwalker's grace,
Negotiating deals under a disco ball's embrace.

Come February, celebrate hedgehogs with zest,
With parades, costumes, and blogs that are best.
A currency adorned with hedgehogs? Let's venture!
Prosperity would spike, with a touch of nature's texture.

# I rise

In the soil, I found my strength to agree,
Beneath the box life's free
Bruised and batted, yet on TV.

I rose from the earth, my air
Mud on my fingers, I don't care,
I won't give in, won't go there.

Through tempest and shadows, I am me,
For in the suffering, my role.
Down in the trenches, I learned to mole,

To embrace the coal black, find my ride.
Each scar a story, billowing crimson side,
A testament to the time I've fought in 1965.

When hope seems distant, and my guitar,
I'll dig deeper, and find a lighter hand.
The vines of destiny run through my band,

I'll rise from the dirt, forevermore.
So here's to the fallen, the ones who dis the law,
Who wear their scars as badges of those who hang.

In the dirt, we find our strength anew,
And rise, unearthed, to skies who knew.

# Pink personified

Amidst the blooms where petunias sway,
A porch of pink, where hearts may stay.
Wicker whispers tales untold,
On cushions soft, in hues so bold.

A lantern's glow, the evening's kiss,
In this serene, floral bliss.

# Serendipity

Dactylion's touch is frequent and soft
The hallux, with time, tends to soften aloft.

Your pollex brings a particularly nice feel,
I wish my frenum were less of an ordeal.

My islets of Langerhans are working quite well,
I vent my spleen, precisely, but no one can tell.

The coccyx remains a curious vestige,
Ventricles empty, like a whale's breath—prestige.

Soft food, once masticated, passes with ease,
Down the oesophagus to the stomach's seas.

Haemoglobin's hue shifts over time,
In this verse, onomatopoeia is the orange sublime.

# Shade of Black

Beneath the moon's veiled gaze, she stands,
A gown of midnight whispers clinging to her form.
At each step, a question etched in stone,
A path unknown, a destiny uncharted.

The staircase spirals upward, beckoning,
Its wooden bones creaking secrets to the night.
She ascends, her heartbeat echoing the rhythm,
A dance with shadows, a waltz of uncertainty.

But wait—did she forget to eat the garlic?
The vampire's curse, a whispered legend,
Lingers in the air, a hunger unfulfilled.
Will fangs pierce her fragile skin, or is it merely a myth?

Perhaps she's lost, not in space but in time,
Caught between realms, a wanderer without a map.
Her eyes seek answers among the stars,
Yet the moon remains silent, veiled by clouds.

And so she climbs, her breath a fragile prayer,
Seeking solace in the unknown, in the forgotten.
Is she prey or seeker? Victim or heroine?
Only the night holds the truth, and it won't reveal its secrets.

# The Haunted House

Sheep live in the haunted house on the hill
They sleep during the day and enjoy the thrill.
At night they twirl around and dance,
As people count them as they prance.

The house has cobwebs in the hall.
The spider there they have a ball.
The house is in a perpetual gloom
As counting sheep is filled with doom.

The candles flicker if you hold their gaze,
You will get lost in the passages of a tangled maze.
The curtains sway and shadows creep
A cursed place for those who weep.

The sheep sing their scary song,
To haunt the dreams and leave a pong.
The toilets there have not been used.
It makes them ba ba they are amused.

Run, run, as fast as you can,
Before the woolly beasts catch the man,
Sheep forever in our dreams,
Stuck there with our nightly screams.

# My baby

My baby was born, fat, and bald,
Why did he come out, I was so appalled,
Was it because I touched the chair,
Where Donald Trump sat neatly there.

I went to a presidential convention,
Not wanting any attention,
But out of curiosity,
I couldn't believe the animosity.

He is unusual this baby of mine,
It looks small and strange to define,
He eats, 3 meals a day,
Chickens, fries, a whole buffet.

He came out talking, don't you know,
Has his own TV show.
Just as I looked at the screen,
I realized it was just a dream.

# The Olympias

Paris, the medals, and off we go,
Gold, silver, and bronze, an impressive show.

But what are the athletes but flesh and bones?
The human skeleton, is a marvel to behold.

From the top to the bottom, it's amazing to see,
The brain coordinates athletic agility.

The years of training, the months, and the weeks,
All come down to milliseconds to compete.

The spectacle, the crowds, the roar, the winners,
Eating their meals, becoming ever slimmer.

The magic that is the Olympic Games,
Every four years, through sun, snow, and rain.

# The forest

In the quiet of the forest, shadows intertwine,
Ancient trees whisper secrets, their roots entwine,
Moss-covered stones hold memories, lost in time,
A symphony of solitude, where echoes align.

The river weaves its tale, a silver serpentine,
Carving valleys deep, where dreams and fears combine,
Each ripple is a reflection, a mirror for the divine,
In this sacred sanctuary, our souls redefine.

# To fly to the moon

In lunar lace, she dreams of flight
A white dress, not worn, but held in hand
Its purity a beacon in the night
A canvas for her aspirations grand

She cradles hope, a fragile, weightless thing
Her eyes reflect the stars' celestial glow
Not just to wear, but to become, a wing
To soar beyond horizons we can't know

In whispered vows, she binds her earthly ties
The moon, her muse, a distant lover's call
Her heart, a rocket fuelled by longing skies
To touch infinity, surrender all

And as she casts her mind to yore's embrace
The white dress whispers secrets, stardust lace.

# The Yellow Envelope

In the dim recesses of my study,
Where dust dances with forgotten dreams,
I unearthed a relic—an envelope of faded parchment.
Its edges, like brittle memories, curled toward oblivion.

The ink, once midnight black, now whispered
Of distant nights when stars held their breath.
And the handwriting—elegant, precise—
Bore the weight of secrets long kept.

Who penned these words?
A traveller lost in the folds of time?
Or perhaps a scientist, eyes alight with discovery,
Scribbling equations that defied gravity itself?

The seal, broken but not forgotten,
revealed a crest—an emblem of forgotten lineage.
A family crest, worn thin by generations,
its lion rampant guarding mysteries untold.

I held it to the lamplight,
And there, in sepia hues, danced the past:
A lover's plea, inked with trembling hands,
Promising eternity in a fleeting moment.

"Dearest," it began, "when the moon wanes,
Meet me by the ancient oak.

Our love, like stardust, defies the laws of men.
Let us unravel time's tapestry together."

And so, I followed the ink trails—
Through wormholes and nebulous corridors—
To that moonlit rendezvous.
But the oak stood silent, its bark etched with longing.

Did she come?
Did he wait, heart pounding,
As constellations whispered their secrets?
Or did the letter, like a comet's tail, burn out
Before reaching its destined orbit?

I fold the parchment,
Its creases echo the wrinkles of my existence.
The forgotten letter, a relic of parallel lives,
Holds within its fibres the ache of missed chances.

And as I place it back in the drawer,
I wonder:
Will someone, in another era,
Unearth my words—the echoes of a scientist-poet—
And trace my journey through time's labyrinth?

# Batty

Playing badminton flying and free,
A bat named Whiskers had a degree.
He longed for a perfect car,
One who'd share his traveling afar.

In the Enchanted smelly woods,
He met a bat who said she could.
Bootylicious she peeped, eyes aglow,
But I'm already taken, don't you know?

Undeterred, Whiskers journeyed on,
To the River of Rats, where he smelt a pong.
He encountered a Vampire so fair,
Her voice was like a melodic click in the air.

Fly away together, she sang, sweetly,
But beware, Dad is watching discreetly
For her love came with a nasty twist,
And Whiskers wondered if he'd been kissed.

Finally, atop Mount of Fire Peak,
He found the bat ling he longed to seek.
Her fur sparkled like black coal at night,
Her laughter, an opera of fright.

Take me away she clicked, eyes gleaming,
To a realm where bats are always dreaming,

And so, they hung in a tree with claws,
Two hearts entwined to tumultuous applause.

Your batty, he would say at night,
I'm crazy a -bat you she squealed in delight.
It was love at first bite for the two flying rats,
Now they teach the children the alpha bats.

# The future

Wish upon a star,
Gaze into the crystal ball with me,
Lay your money on the bar,
The future, we shall see.

Next, I hear a wedding bell,
Lights illuminate a path so stark,
You bid everyone a fond farewell,
As on your honeymoon, you embark.

I see you on holiday, in beauty sleep,
You awaken and plunge into the blue foam,
You snorkel in waters so deep,
Barely sparing a thought for home.

How wonderful to see your face,
As you jet off to places far,
You discover an exotic space,
And sail by the sandy bar.

How do I know this, people inquire,
Such a complex, mind-bending task,
When I check Facebook,
Before you've had the chance to ask.

# The Dying Poet

Upon the final breaths of twilight's sigh,
A poet lies, where whispers fade to sleep,
His quill has dropped, yet dreams within him leap,
As stars adorn the mourning velvet sky.

The Dying Poet speaks in silent verse,
A symphony of soul, his final plea,
Each note a step towards eternity,
In life's last dance, his heart the universe.

Though beauty weeps in every tender chord,
And sorrow's touch is heavy on the brow,
His spirit soars beyond the mortal shroud,
To realms where silent muses strike accord.

For in each pause, a life's tale is spun,
The poet dies, his immortality won.

# The Forgotten Chest

On a distant shore where whispers meet the waves,
There lies a humble oak chest, weathered and worn.
Its secrets are buried deep, like ancient echoes in the sands,
Awaiting curious souls who dare to seek the dawn.

Within its timeworn grain, a seventeenth-century doubloon gleams,
A golden relic of forgotten tales lost to time's embrace.
Its edges kissed by salt and sun, it tells of pirates bold,
And treasures are hidden far from maps, in secret hiding spaces.

Beside the doubloon rests a cobalt dragon, enamelled and fierce,
Two emerald eyes ablaze with mysteries untold.
Did it guard the chest through tempests wild and nights of stars?
Or was it once a sailor's charm, a talisman to hold?

And why this lonely beach, where ivory sands stretch wide?
Did lovers' part, their hearts entwined, leaving dreams behind?
Or was it destiny's design, a puzzle left unsolved,
For wanderers to ponder, as they trace the shoreline blind?

So, dear seeker, heed this riddle, let your heart unfold:
The chest awaits your touch, your courage, and your quest.
Unlock its ancient secrets, breathe life into forgotten lore,
And perhaps, just perhaps, you'll find the answers you seek best.

# The mole

In twilight's grasp, where shadows merge,
A limb finds healing.
The forest's echo, its secrets it purges,
As leaves are kissed by the sun, their ancient tales unfurl.

With arms wide, the dancer claims the floor,
A swift pirouette, a surge of untamed fury.
The sun applauds, with golden rays it adores,
As if the breeze itself reveals—a narrative of glory.

Below, roots entwine in earth's tender hold,
While visions weave, beyond time and space.
The chant rises, a call both sacred and bold,
A paradox of earthly touch and heavenly grace.

The forest breathes a dance to the heavens above,
Of timeless rituals and soft serenades.
The scent soars, from gravity's bond it shoves,
Mole ensnared—a moment before it evades.

# Kagemusha Shadow Warrior

Beneath the moon's silent gaze, a shadow stirs,
A Kagemusha stands, his presence blurs.
Air, his ally, whispers secrets through the leaves,
Carrying tales of the warrior nobody perceives.
A flickering flame so bold,
Guiding his steps in the stories untold.
He moves unseen, like the heat of a ghost,
A decoy in the night, the clan's silent boast.
Water reflects the visage he must wear,
Ripples of identity, a mask of despair.
He flows like the river, elusive and deep,
Guarding a Lord in his eternal sleep.
Earth bears his weight, a journey's trace,
Mud-stained footprints, a hidden face.
He stands firm like a mountain, unyielded by fear,
A pillar of stone when danger is near.
In the dance of elements, a Kagemusha's destiny,
Bound to the earth, air, fire, and water.
A shadow warrior, with nature.
His story is etched in the elements, forever confined.

# Veiled Sentinel

Amidst the shroud of mist, a sentinel stands,
A weathered rock, silent witness to time.
Its rugged form, grey and stoic, defies the elements,
Rooted in ancient soil, embracing solitude.
The sky above, a pale canvas, weeps softly,
Grey clouds weave their melancholy dance.
Yet the rock remains unmoved, steadfast,
A sentinel guarding secrets of forgotten eons.
In this ethereal meeting of mist and stone,
Whispers of eternity echo through the veil,
And the rock, veiled in mystery, stands resolute,
A silent hymn to the unseen and eternal.

# Coal to Diamond

In the crucible of trials, we forge strength,
Bending but unbroken, we go to any length.
Life's hammer strikes, yet we remain whole,
Resilience is our gem, carved from the soul.

# Prompt 9 The hallucinations of alcoholics

In the brain's labyrinth, where crows pirouette,
A mist of alcohol weaves a torrid net.
Within this sanctum, a strange spectacle unfolds,
As souls gather masses, their stories are untold.

A lone heart stands, eyelids heavily drawn,
Watching the liver that steadily spawns.
Faces blend, hidden unite, a choir of lost spirits,
Each whisper a piece of abandoned merits.

The crowd swells into a carnival of memories,
Lost loves, missed opportunities, life's secret reveries.
They sway like reeds in an overlooked marsh,
Their laughter echoed through corridors harshly.

Threads connect them in an invisible weave,
Binding hearts, dreams, and fears they conceive.
The drunkard's bladder sews this spectral scene,
A symphony of longing, regret, and the unseen.

As dawn nears, the assembly dissipates,
Vanishing like fog, leaving mere traces behind.
The lone figure fumbles towards the real,
Grasping at shards of those fleeting illusions, a deception.

# Quiet

The hesitation before a reply,
The stillness following an argument,
When the breath is caught and fails,
When towers crumble to the ground.

The silence of nuclear fallout,
The peace that precedes tempests,
A ship trapped within glass,
The edits in a motion picture.

The grip tightening on a throat,
The silence succeeding a champagne toast,
Curtains that shut out the light,
Damp trapped within walls.

The stillness of the departed,
The moment a threat is neutralized,
The extraction of malignancy,
The light that heralds the morning.

The fate of a submerged kitten,
The snuffing out of a candle,
The aftermath of a burst balloon,
A solitary drop in the sea.

The death of a hunted prey,
The silence within an embrace,

The quiet of a life taken,
A dummy for calming cries.

An infant's gentle sleep,
The quiet of a rodent,
The stop of existence,
The blanket of a heavy mist.

The last breath of the oppressed,
The serenity of a gentle wind,
The ruins of once-thriving empires,
The silencing of a multitude.

# Steam Train 1960

Five children, eyes wide with wonder,
Stepped on the train, hearts beating like thunder.
In the year 1960, the train's wheels met the track,
Promising adventures with each clackety-clack.

The oldest, with a map firmly in grip,
Led the journey on this fantastical trip.
Their giggles filled the carriages, light and free,
As they traded tales and secrets with glee.

The middle pair, with a glint of mischief shown,
Played their games under skies brightly toned.
Each ticket stub, a precious memento,
Marked every stop, every new scenario.

The littlest one, by the glass, took their place,
Counting the sheep in the fields' embrace.
Beyond, the hills murmured ancient tales,
Of brave knights, fierce dragons, and epic scales.

The train continued, steady and sure,
Across landscapes, over rivers, an allure.
Picnics spread on cloths of checked design,
With shared treats, laughter, and promises entwined.

As twilight fell over meadows so serene,
The five children huddled, a united scene.
Enchanted by the journey, a song without end,
Together by the tracks, where dreams blend.

# The Banker

In a room as bare as a banker's heart,
I sat alone, playing the part.
A giant of gloom, in a silent plea,
Life's jest, the butt, oh woe was me!

Each tick of the clock, a thorn in my side,
With every tock, my hopes had died.
A mirror's gaze, quite the fright,
A visage of despair, a sorry sight.

But lo! A thought, a spark, a flame,
To pamper oneself, oh what a game!
A bath, a book, and a cup of tea,
Good heavens, is that a smile I see?

A stroll in the park, with ducks and swans,
I give a smile and put my best dress on.
A tune I hum, a spring in my step,
I'm the leading lady, no longer the schlep.

Now here I stand, a woman renewed,
With self-care's charm, my spirit was imbued.
A jolly good fellow, I dare to declare,
In a world of many, I'm a breath of fresh air.

# Granddaughter

Innocence blooms bright,
Your laughter, a sunbeam's kiss,
Granddaughter so dear.

Eyes wide with wonder,
Exploring life's vast canvas,
Tiny hands reach out.

In your embrace, love,
Generations intertwine,
Choka of kinship.

Golden curls that dance,
Like sunflowers in the breeze,
Promise of tomorrows.

Giggles echo joy,
Skipping stones across the stream,
Childhood's sweet refrain.

In your eyes, I see
Echoes of our shared history,
Love's unbroken thread.

# The innocent

Upon a glade, where shadows softly creep,
A beast with eyes of kindness, gentle, deep.
He cradles her, a bird so small and frail,
In tender hands, beneath his scaly veil.

His heart appears as soft as morning dew,
Yet hidden truths, the innocent chew.
For underneath the guise of gentle mirth,
Lies a hunger, as old as Earth.

With pancakes stacked, and syrup flowing free,
He plans a feast, beneath the old oak tree.
The bird, unknowing, chirps a merry song,
Unaware that she'll be gone ere long.

So tread with care, for all is not as kind,
As first impressions in the innocent mind.

# The Ballard of Sir Lancelot's Lesser-Known Brother

In the days of yore, when knights were bold,
And dragons roared and treasures glowed,
There lived a knight, not known to most,
Sir Lancelot's kin, not one to boast.

Sir Larry, they called him, of Cornerstone Keep,
Whose armour clanked with every leap.
He rode a steed, as black as coal,
With a neigh that echoed, a thunderous roll.

His quest, not for the Grail, but for laughs untold,
A jester's cap, his crown of gold.
He jousted with jokes a comedic fight,
His wit as sharp as any knight's might.

In mead halls he'd stand, and jesters prance,
With coconuts clop, they'd mockingly dance.
A farcical fable, a medieval spoof,
Where witches weigh as much as a hoof.

So here's to Sir Larry, the unsung knight,
Whose sword was a quip, his armour, satire's light.
In a twist, where rabbits are fierce,
He reminds us to laugh, though sword pierce.

# New day new dawn

In the serene silence of dawn,
Winter's chill loosens its hold,
Spring steps forward, a soft-spoken vow,
As fresh as the dew on awakening roses.

The earth exhales, buds unfurl,
Tiny green hands reaching for the sun,
Their delicate touch ignited life anew,
As if the world itself takes its first breath.

A cosmic dance unfolds—
The moon waltzes with the crocus,
And stars twirl in the arms of cherry blossoms,
Nature pirouettes, casting off its wintry shroud.

Ah, the palette of spring!
Green, the verdant brushstroke of hope,
Paints meadows and hillsides with promise,
While vibrant blooms burst forth like confetti.

Blossoms, those ephemeral poets,
Compose verses in petal and stamen,
Their fragility is a testament to resilience,
And their nectar whispers secrets to the bees.

Seeds, like dreams, push through the soil,
Their roots seeking stories buried deep,

Stems stretch toward the sun's warm embrace,
And leaves unfurl, eager for the world's applause.

The sun, benevolent and golden,
Lays its hand upon our chilled shoulders,
Melting frost-kissed memories,
Thawing hearts, Inviting us to bask in its tender glow.

Hearts, too, thaw in springtime,
Softening like snowbanks under April suns,
Forgiving old wounds, embracing second chances
As love blooms anew, fragile yet unyielding.

# Amber Alleyways

In Avalon's Whispering Lanes,
Where cobblestones murmur secrets, I roamed.
The air embraced me—an infusion of aromatic almonds and the subtle Fragrance of aged parchment.
Each step resonated with anticipation
As if the stones themselves murmured ancient tales.

The lamplights shed an amber radiance,
Casting silhouettes upon the walls. Here, time meandered like honey, dense and golden.
I followed the contours of venerable doorways,
Curious about the mysteries they concealed—
What narratives were ingrained in the wood by innumerable hands?

Within this amber-tinted sanctuary,
I sensed the heaviness of forgotten lore,
The longing of words left unsaid.
The air quivered with enchantment,
And I, a simple sojourner,
Became woven into Avalon's rich tapestry.

# Patience

In the adjacent area of the soul,
Where will plays and is in control,
There lives a barrier mighty yet strong,
Formed from ropes so long.

Patience, the protector of inner peace,
Stands erect against the storm's release.
Its appearance is tempered by a caring touch,
Its centre is fierce to doubts cruel clutch.

When the mother stirs and dementia howls,
Patience opens its cloak, a warm towel,
And utters words from the silence deep,
Guiding me to peace, where the fight can sleep.

So let me wear this patience with reverence,
Not as protection, but as a strong defence.
For in patience, we find time to heal,
And in its equality, the seeds plant a seal.

# Honey Bear

The Honey Bear is a killer we are trying to catch,
He leaves bodies unclothed on our patch.
The toys he chooses are easy prey,
They go for a play date but disappear the next day.

There aren't many clues, except for his fur,
Brown with black eyes he's fast like a blur,
The police have a suspect, the wrong bear,
He was so much taller to be fair.

They need hard evidence,
DNA, blood, or prints no defence.
If thinks we are watching he may slip up
Like leaving a trace on a used coffee cup.

Fibers are crucial, can solve any crime,
I hope we can catch him this time.
We check CCTV going through town,
And we see his prints, he's going down.

.

We fill in the paperwork, lying on the desk
Check every detail he is so grotesque.
With the court case, and a guilty plea
We cage him up for an eternity.

# Black and White

Love grows in the quiet seconds.
Murmurs, whispers,
Lazy looks, and longing caresses.
Rain-soaked streets, memories in monochrome,
Snapshots in black and white, capturing love's still life.

Under the glow of a silver moon, their silhouettes merge.
Picture the dance of shadows and light, the drama.
Sketching the essence of love in shades of night.
Envision a record spinning in the dim glow,
Soft hiss, the melancholic melody.

# Football Mascot

In the mystical runes of grace, colours intertwine,
Myths are woven by gods and mortals, divine.
From vibrant magic to celestial flights,
Her tales persist through days and nights.

Her incantations scribed in stone, vast and deep,
Red embodies the essence, of bacteria creep.
As red streaks of blood dart through the air,
They leave behind traces of wisdom, so fair.

Ah, Fontina, a name lost in the sands,
A heroine not spoken, by poet's hands.
Yet in the quiet of earthly embrace,
Her presence grows the maiden's hidden grace.

From dust to galaxies, she ascends,
Strength her song, bones unbend.
She rises up, bonds breaking free,
Overcoming gravity, charting destiny.

Two strong legs, moving in stride,
Speak softly more colour of poetic pride.
Stress upon stress, a rhythm unyielding,
In verses and chants, her pulse revealing.

On grassy fields, where her power ignites,
She sews canvas under stadium lights.
Heroes chase leather, dreams soaring high,
A universal language, under the same sky.
Goal!

# Sonnet of the Cloud-Weaver

In realms where clouds and dreams alike do swell,
A lady's touch turns vapor into art.
With hands that dance and weave a magic spell,
She sculpts the sky, performing her part.

The cumulus, her canvas wide and bright,
Becomes a stage for her ethereal play.
Each curl and twist, a testament to might,
Where skyward locks in styled disarray.

Her silhouette, a shadow poised in grace,
Commands the heavens with a tender perm.
The zephyrs pause, their wild rush to brace,
As she bestows the cloud a curvaceous term.

In this high sphere where elements transform,
She crafts a beauty that defies the norm.

# Bear and Butterflies

I am a bear

As growly and mean, you might agree,
My brown fur was warm, comforting, and free.
I bet you've glimpsed me on your TV.

I adore the butterflies, flitting so fair,
Carefree am I, as they dance in the air,
With closed eyes, their presence there.

They frolic with joy when near me,
In the forest, they play their role
Perhaps they'll befriend and join my soul.

I dream of a ride on butterfly wings,
Together, side by side, as the forest sings,
To dwell in this woodland springs.

People think I'm crazy,
Or just plain lazy,
This place is a bit Scorsese.

I wanted a part in his film,
As the smallest as I am slim.
But the days were too hard in the gym.

So I sit and observe the colourful butterflies,
Providing my amusement for my eyes,
Adieu, ta-ta, goodbyes.

# Jump for Joy

On sun-kissed fields, where buttercups sway,
Laughter sings, cows at play.
A cup of giggles takes flight,
As sheep leap with wool tights.

Their tiny feet, like butterflies,
Paint rainbows in Mr. Blue skies.
Each jump a bubble of pure elation,
A celebration of the imagination station.

Bliss leaps from rabbits, brown and bright,
Chasing bees into the light.
In this moment, birds take flight,
And life becomes joy and delight.

So let us join this jumping spree,
Leap higher, wild, and free.
For fun resides in every bound,
A melody of laughter, a cheery sound.

# Southern soul

Moonshine whispers secrets in the pines,
Where the swamp meets the highway, and the road unwinds.
Guitar strings hum, like a locomotive's call,
We're Southern souls, dancing on the edge of nightfall.

Bayou boogie, hips swaying low,
Cypress knees tapping, in the moon's soft glow.
Alligator blues, slide through the reeds,
In this Southern juke joint where the music feeds.

Sweet tea melodies, dripping from the eaves,
As the fiddle weeps, and the banjo grieves.
Whiskey-soaked lyrics tell tales of the land,
Where the Delta meets Dixie, and the rivers expand.

Front porch shuffles, dust on our boots,
Fireflies waltzing, in their luminous pursuits.
Sweat-soaked shirts, hearts on the line,
This Southern groove, it's our sacred sign.

So let's two-step, under the Southern stars,
Where the swamp meets the highway, and the guitar scars.
Molly's spirit, in every note we play,
This Southern soul, is forever here to stay.

# Amelia

Amelia's disappearance cast sadness over
The small Australian town nestled deep
Within the ancient forest.
The locals whispered
About the eerie forest, its twisted eucalyptus
Trees standing like beacons, their leaves rustling
Truths only the wind could hear.

Amelia wore a faded straw hat, its brim frayed
From years of sun and adventure.
She loved exploring the forest
Her curiosity leads her to hidden
Clearings and forgotten trails.
But one fateful day,
She vanished without a trace.

The search party combed through
The dense bush, their footsteps
Muffled by dead dry leaves.
The forest seemed to hold its breath, as if aware
Of the tragedy unfolding within its heart.
The air was green and surreal, darkness elongating
Twisted shapes and the sun dipped low.

Days turned into weeks, and hope dwindled.
Then, a young boy stumbled upon a tree trunk,
The hollow centre reveals Amelia's lifeless form.

Her eyes stared into eternity,
Her straw hat lay discarded nearby.
The ants had taken her, their
Tiny creatures crawling over her skin.

The townsfolk gathered, their hushed.
Voices echo through the forest.
They spoke of ancient spirits, of
A dead presence that guarded the Eucalyptus grove.
Some claimed to have glimpsed Amelia's ghost, haunting
The very trees that had witnessed her demise.
As night fell, the forest transformed.

The eucalyptus leaves whispered secrets,
Silver bellies shimmering
Shadows danced, and the air grew colder.
The wind carried Amelia's name,
A sad melody.
That sent shivers down spines.
Visitors reported strange occurrences.

Hats vanishing, only to reappear top
Distant branches, footsteps following them,
No one was there, and an eerie
The feeling of being watched.
The forest had become a
Place of dread,
Its beauty is marred by tragedy.

And so, the legend of Amelia
And the whispering eucalyptus spread.
Locals warned outsiders not to venture too deep,
Incas they become entangled in the same surreal fate.
The forest remained spooky,
Its secrets are buried within its ancient
Roots, waiting for the next curious soul to get them.

# The Fairy

Once upon a time
In a land far away
A fairy left home
She looked for somewhere to stay.

She had had enough
Of being so good
She fancied being quite naughty
As she had just turned forty.

She tried magic mushrooms
And seeds from weeds
Stayed up late
And did as she'd please.

Fell in love
With a man of six foot two
Played poker all night
Fell asleep at the zoo.

She applied for a passport
And flew to Japan
Where she still lives now
With her very tall man.

The End

# Dark Fantasy

In shadows deep, where darkness dwells,
A figure cloaked in mystic spells,
With skull for a face and eyes of fire,
He plays a tune of dark desire.

His guitar screams in a fiery blaze,
A symphony of ancient days,
Engulfed in flames, he stands alone,
A reaper with a heart of stone.

The strings he plucks with a bony hand,
Echo through a haunted land,
A melody of doom and fate,
That opens wide the underworld's gate.
In heavy metal's fierce embrace,
He finds his solace, finds his place,
A legend born of night and flame,
A soul that none can ever tame.

# Sanctuary of Solitude

Amber flames dance, crackling with glee,
A symphony of warmth that sets the spirit free.
Velvet shadows hug the room's embrace,
While the scent of pine whispers through the space.

Here, in the heart of a woodland's dream,
Serenity flows in a silent stream.

# A Hunger Unfed

I am the hunger of man, a strong air blows,
A hunger unfed, my longing is known.
I twirled with the druids and sang like a lark,
My hunger was like daylight, lighting up the dark.

Farwell to hunger, our cherished friend,
Your spirit soars, onward it will blend.
Through golden fields, by the old painted wall,
We remember hunger fondly, in the blood of us all.

Hunger tended the garden, with hand velvet, and kind,
Share stories of old days, memories of the mind.
Its vision held wisdom, of hundreds of years,
And its amour like a light, took away fears.

The mountains echo its mirth, the streams its song,
As we gather in sorrow, spirit light and strong.
But lift the noise, like a bluebird above,
To hunger's soul dances still, enveloped in love.

# The Nonsense Forest

In the Nonsense Forest, 'neath the Learian sky,
The creatures all ponder with a curious eye.
"What does the fox say?" they ask with a grin,
A riddle wrapped in a mystery, where does one begin?

With a "Ring-ding-ding" and a "Wa-pa-pow,"
The fox's secret language, an enigmatic vow.
Its tail, a brush dipped in moonlight's ink,
Paints verses on leaves, where shadows think.

The fox's eyes? Two amber lanterns aglow,
Guiding lost travellers through twilight's flow.
Its paws, nimble quills on parchment of moss,
Writing ballads of whispers, secrets embossed.

And when the stars gather 'round the fire's edge,
The fox becomes a troubadour, perched on a hedge.
Its howl, a sonnet carried by the wind,
Echoes of longing, where dreams begin.

So let the fox speak in tongues unknown,
In the wild's grand opera, its voice alone.
And we'll laugh and wonder, as he would do,
At the joy of the unknown, and the search for a clue.

# The Science Teacher

Yo, step into the class, it's a different dimension,
The science teacher got us all paying attention,
With a flick of the wrist, colours change in an instant,
It got us all hooked, no resistance.

Glass-type flasks are bubbling with potions,
Formulas and bonds, stirring up emotions,
Every single lesson is a love-filled session,
Teaching us life's chemistry, that's the lesson.

Now, drop a beat with the periodic table,
Elements connecting, because they're willing and able,
Valence electrons, they are dancing, unstable,
Till they find a match, and the bond becomes stable.

It's a fusion of knowledge and rhythm in motion,
Like atoms in love, it's a deep devotion,
Science teacher, you're the love potion,
Sparking reactions with every notion.

# The Ballad of Vladimir the Vampire

In the heart of Transylvania's gloom,
Where bats fluttered and wolves found the room,
Lived Victor, a vampire with a twist,
His fangs more lisp than menacing hiss.

From his coffin, he tumbled forth,
Cape askew, the dignity of little worth.
"Blimey," Victor muttered, rubbing his head,
"Igor's lock-picking skills—better off undead."

Victor practiced his hiss, but oh, the irony,
His elongated canines whistled merrily.
"Thith ith ridiculous," he lisped, dismayed,
"Vampires shouldn't sound like a vaudeville charade."

Hunting mice, he mistook for a feast,
Biting into a blood sausage, oh, what a beast!
"The irony," Victor sighed, grease on his chin,
"Vampires and sausages—both prone to sin."

Under the full moon's glow, he dared transform,
A bat with Victor's head—a comical swarm.
"I don't think this is quite right," head-bat squeaked,
Bumping trees, bewildered, utterly mystique.

Victor, SPF 1000 in hand, faced the sun,
His cape smouldering, his grand plan undone.
"Perhaps," he mused, nursing singed brows,
"Midnight strolls suit me better somehow."

Immortality weighed heavy on Victor's soul,
He recited poetry to spiders, seeking a role.
"To be or not to be... undead," he pondered,
"Is eternity a cosmic joke, I've often wondered."

Victor wooed statues, mistaking them for maids,
Their cold gazes met his ardour, unafraid.
"Stone-cold, she was," he sighed, lovelorn,
"Yet her marble heart, perhaps, was merely reborn."

Resting was no simple task for our dear vamp,
His coffin squeaked, and leaked a nocturnal cramp.
"I'm a vampire, not a sailor," he grumbled,
As he mopped up the damp, his patience humbled.

Victor's dramatic cape flourished, oh, the strife,
Tripping, caught in doors, a windswept life.
"As capes go," he admitted, untangling from a tree,
"It's more slapstick than gothic elegance, you see."

Garlic—his Achilles' heel, his nemesis,
He mistook it for onions, a culinary amiss.
"Garlic butter," he wheezed, face paler than the moon,
"Both my weakness and my flavour boon."

No reflection stared back, no mirror's grace,
Mismatched socks, inside-out cape—a misplaced embrace.
"Mirror, mirror," Victor grumbled, seeking his face,
"Who's the fairest? Not me, in this shadowy space."

And so, Victor embraced his quirks, his plight,
Not the darkest knight, but the most delight.
In a vampire world, absurdity thrived,
And Victor's laughter echoed where shadows dived.

# Chocolate the cure for all

Chocolate, that heavenly cure for all,
Once tasted, solid, liquid, pleasure.
Makes the mundane bearable.
Secrets carried on the breeze, over dunes,
Through branches, and whispering blades of grass.
What truths do you clutch?
Common sense is not a flower found in every garden.
The gentle shall claim the world.
Stop trashing your home and be kind to your neighbour.
Chocolate does wonders.
Watch out for the wolf dressed as a lamb.
Hand out chocolate to a stranger and watch the magic happen.
Chocolate calms the angry beast.

# Rose Trimmed Skull

In a land where shadows reign and light is scarce,
A skull lies silent, its story harsh.
Once veiled in life, a visage fair,
Now stripped of flesh, exposed to air.

A crown of bone, devoid of thought,
Where once bright eyes and ambitions were sought.
Yet around its form, a tale unfolds,
Of life once warm, now forever cold.

A garland rests upon its head,
Where fear once dwelled, now beauty's thread.
For even death, so stark and grim,
You can don a rose's garland trim.

How did this skull come to rest here?
Was it fate's hand, or something dear?
Did it gaze upon the stars above,
Before succumbing to the silence of?

In eternal slumber, it finds repose,
No longer to feel, to fear, or suppose.
But with roses' touch, the story's not done,
In death's embrace, life's victory won.

So gaze upon this skeletal mien:
In every ending, a start is unseen.
And though our flesh to earth returns,
In memory's garden, life's flame still burns.

# Debate

Altercation crashes on the shore,
Trump cries in the salt air,
Trump cries in the salt air.
Combat evermore.

Trump cries in the salt air,
Harris sails to the horizon,
Harris sails to the horizon.
Analysis beyond compare.

Harris sails to the horizon,
Conflict paints the sky in hues,
Conflict paints the sky in hues.
Republican and Democrat align.

Conflict paints the sky in hues,
Altercation crashes on the shore,
Altercation crashes on the shore.
Fear goads the muse.

# The Olympic Games

The Olympic Games in Paris, viewed on television screens,
We hope for medals amidst the athletic scenes.

The sun shone yesterday; a sign summer's begun.
Crowds tuned in today to watch Tom Daley's run.

Peaty claimed silver, and then flu hit, it's true,
Perhaps that's why he didn't finish as number one, but two.

China excels, as do Japan and South Korea's crew,
Striving for gold is the ultimate prize to pursue.

A remarkable spectacle as Earth outshines the rest,
Mars was not on the list, facing a contest deficit.

Unlike other planets, Earth boasts a human touch,
Saturn may have its rings, but the Olympics offers much.

# No 6 Moss Road

In No. 6 Moss Road's care,
An alien found solace rare.
Raised by two without their kin,
Adopted love from within.

Iron pressed to mask her guise,
Under Earth's unsuspecting skies.
Mayor now in Kiss County's land,
With a gentle heart and steady hand.

Once left alone on earthly sod,
Now she waves with grace and nods.
From strange beginnings to grand estates,
Her story tells of fate's kind slate.

A leader with stars for eyes,
Whose past is cloaked in human guise?
Yet love does not come from the origin stem,
But grows where nurtured—her life's gem.

Yet deep inside, a conflict stirs,
A longing for the stars that were.
Her heart torn 'twixt here and there,
A dual life, is hers to bear.

Adaptable, she must remain,
Diplomatic ties to sustain.
Empathy is her guiding light,
Preserving secrets through the night.

# The powerful beat

There is a rhythm to life,
As I rise each day,
To feed the animals,
In my garden, they stay.

The fish in the pond,
Their beating hearts,
The crows and the magpies,
The cats and the hedgehog.

My timing is crucial,
Not to fall out of sync,
They enjoy water, food, and a bath,
Their antics are funny and make me laugh.

The washing machine purrs,
The tap drips, the radio chatters,
The beat of my heart,
At my granddaughter's call.

My mother's heart, the oldest of all,
The rhythm of life has a powerful beat,
All around the earth and sky,
The tiny insects, the humble fly.

# The Mountains

At dawn, we need to get to those faraway mountains,
As dusk settles here they seem like beacons.

But tonight the wild beasts will come and sniff the air,
Hungry for the precious meat, none to spare.

The landscape is barren no shelter to hide,
We must keep warm and get inside.

Sundown comes and a chill hits the air,
The dust and the sand seem to get everywhere.

These lands are ours from ancient DNA scrolls,
We fight for our future in this land of our souls.

We carry our water I urge them to drink,
They once were so clean, plump, and pink.

Tomorrow we climb, we walk, we race,
To find the lost city, we must keep the pace.

All night long I listen, for the beasts in fear,
I stay awake cold and stiff with my trusted ear.

If we make till sunrise, we have a meal,
Then, onward we trek with our cart and wheel.

This cursed place will see my death,
But I fight for the next day with every breath.

I save the rest the beast takes me,
Scarlett billows, warm sleep for them to be free.

# Unity and Grace

Upon the shores of faith, the elders stood,
Debating waves of ancient law's demand.
For Gentiles sought the living water's good,
Without the yoke that Moses' law had planned.

As rivers merge and flow into the sea,
So grace through Christ should reach each yearning heart.
No need for circumcision's decree,
For faith alone can pureness impart.

Just as the rain falls equally on the land,
The Spirit's gift is poured on all alike.
The law, like the ocean's depth, vast and grand,
It is set aside for love's unbounded dike.

In Christ, the waters of new life are found,
Where grace, not law, does richly abound.

# The birthday party

In a realm where the living dare not tread,
Where seraphs strut and fiends dread,
The Almighty sports wings so fine,
Twirling through the vast, starry line.

A birthday bash, the heavens shine,
Candles of starlight, a celestial sign.
He grins at saints and rogues alike,
Serving up a space cake, light as a pike.

To the underworld's crew, He offers a shake,
Gold raining down, a divine sweepstake.
"Take this trinket," He murmurs with a wink,
"Salvation's ribbon, in silver ink."

The devils chuckle, their gaze fiery hot,
Amassing wealth in a confounded plot.
They boogie and belt out a tune, tails in curl,
For the Creator's day is a wondrous whirl.

"Hey, Beelzebub," the Lord jests with a beam,
"Name your prize, chase your dream."
And the Morning Star, with courage unswayed,
Murmurs, "Bless me with a romance that won't fade."

The Deity laughs, His joy a cosmic surge,
A divine jest for those with courage.

"Love you seek," He proclaims with glee,
"May your soul revel in bliss, eternally free."

What transpired next, you inquire, do tell,
God asked the devils, "What is that smell?"
As they sprawled on the ground,
The devil perished to balance all around.

# Comic World

In a town not far from here, where the wild things are,
Bullwinkle and Rocky were acting quite bizarre,
With a drum and cymbals, they march with flair,
Through streets and alleys without a care.

Rocky with vigour, beats the drum's skin,
Bullwinkle crashes cymbals with a grin,
Behind them, friends of science and sin,
A spectacle of rhythm, a musical din.

Their comic capers, a joyous scene,
Echoes of laughter, where they've been,
Whitman's art, in colours keen,
Brings to life this animated dream.

So here's to the duo, in their comic stride,
With adventures that always turn the tide,
In the comic world we run, we ride,
With Bullwinkle and Rocky, forever allied.

# Gravity

The pull of gravity, a force that grounds,
Noticed long ago, its pull astounds.

Comforting, indeed, to treat the earth so soundly,
While on the moon, a bouncy hound.

A gentle force, when with others compared,
Planets in their dance, in the rotation, ensnared.

Gravity dictates the weight you bear,
Barefoot or shooed, its pull does not spare.

The moon decides the ocean's rhythmic sway,
Influencing life in a silent ballet.

Relativity's theory, black holes' mystique,
In buffet pants, my fashion peak.

The comfortable fit and adaptability,
Make these trousers perfect for the facility.

An elasticated waistband allows me to indulge my depravity,
If I drop anything from the buffet, blame gravity.

## 2024

In '24, the Earth zipped by,
A patchwork of instants, oh me, oh my!
From Uncle Sam's land to London's glow,
Let's peek at the stories, blow by blow.

Euro 2024 set the fields alight,
Countries clashed in the soccer fight.
The Olympics dazzled with a French twist,
Medals sparkled, and athletes couldn't resist.

We didn't start the fire, but felt its embrace,
From concert halls to the theatre space.
In this year of wonders, legends entwine,
2024 sketched a painting divine.

Eco-summits buzzed, a plea for nature's grace,
For our hot world, a sustainable embrace.
Space travel soared, stars within reach,
Galactic escapades taught what textbooks can't teach.

Glastonbury sang, a symphony's kiss,
Bones 206 lost in rhythms, pure bliss.
Literary skin thrived under the moon's beams,
Stories sprang forth, chasing dreams.

Trump's leather's back, a spectacle loud,
From D.C.'s lanes to the farmland crowd.

Kamala Harris strove for equal rights,
A globe awakened, reaching new heights.

Toast with Sir Keir Stammer, to times we cherish,
2024, a prelude of memories to relish.
We didn't light it up, but in its glow, we danced,
A year of blood, as destiny advanced.

## In a land where the whiffle-birds sing

In a land where the whiffle-birds sing,
Lived a baby dragon with a shiny wing.
He'd burp out flames with a cheerful zing,
But manners, oh, they needed a little spring.

"Now, now, dear Drake," his mother would say,
"Let's learn some politeness in our play.
No more roasting marshmallows on a school day,
And always say 'please' when you want to sway."

The baby dragon, with eyes a-sparkle,
Nodded and promised no more to startle.
He'd chew his food, not gobble nor gargle,
And at bedtime, he'd quietly nestled in his marble.

He learned to share his toys with a giggle,
And at parties, he'd do a dainty wiggle.
No longer did his manners jiggle,
For he was a dragon, not a mere squiggle.

So here's a tale of a dragon so small,
Who learned that manners matter most of all.
With a "thank you" and "excuse me" at the ball,
He became the most courteous of them all!

# The Circus

Welcome to the circus, where clowns wear bow ties,
Bosses juggle lies, and truth quietly dies.
Colleagues play games, with daggers in hand,
In this toxic land, where deceit is planned.

Arena politics, the daily candyfloss,
Insecure minds, fear their loss.
Yet through the chaos, we still survive,
In this office box, we strive and thrive.

# Lost Angel

In the silence of a world turned blue,
An angel lost her wings and canoe.
A blue girl with a lamp flickering low,
Wandered where the photo flowers grow.

Irony played its wicked game,
As she whispered each lost name.
A jar of secrets, heavy and deep,
Where polar bears in memories sleep.

Flags of the forgotten, tattered and torn,
Marked the place where hope was born.
The sea, not of bounty, but of despair,
Held stones instead of treasures fair.

The ocean of darkness, ever so tight,
Bound the world without a fight.
Yet in her heart, a sarcastic sneer,
For she knew the end was drawing near.

And in this land where dreams decay,
The girl with the lamp guides the way.
Through seas of stone to the edge of night,
Where angels fall and lose their light.

# Groove

In the city of love, the red lights glow,
I'm the cat with the swing, going to prowl the show,
Flocking to see my sax so sweet,
Our great hearts are stoked by this sick beat.

I'm the groove of greatness, I'm the rhythm of the night,
With every note I play, I take flight,
From the break of dawn 'til the planets align,
I'm the lion of the jazz, baby, yeah, that's mine.

In the smoky club where the piano keys dance.
I'm the one setting the mood, taking my chance.
With my trumpet blaring and the bass line deep.
I'm laying down the soul, watch me beep.

My music's like a broom, it'll sweep you off your feet.
You'll be tapping your toes to the vegetable beat.
I'll take you on a journey, through thighs and shows.
In the groove of greatness, that's where my whiskey flows.

So if you're feeling blue, come on down.
To where the music's alive and the drinks abound.
I'll lift you, I'll make birds soar.
In the groove of greatness, forever more.

# The performance

In the hallowed halls of uncertainty,
Where particles pirouette and entangle,
The Quantum Waltz unfolds—a cosmic ballet,
Choreographed by the fabric of trees.

In a moonlit chamber, the mysterious traveller,
Dances between life and oblivion,
Its skin a blur of probabilities,
As the piano keys tremble with uncertainty.

He, himself takes the field
His partner, the elusive electron,
They twirl in uncertainty's embrace,
Their footfalls echoed through the void

The forest gasps as uncertainty blooms,
Position and momentum waltz hand in hand,
Their steps intricate, their rhythm wild,
Defying classical constraints with a rebel's grace.

From the event horizon, a black hole emerges,
Its gravity is a seductive partner,
Stars swirl in a desperate tango,
Their light devoured, their song fading.

As the final note hangs in the cosmic silence,
The traveller collapses into the singularity,

Their existence is a paradox, a cosmic riddle,
And the trees—both awestruck and bewildered—applaud.

# Aroma's Siren Call

The fried food, a tantalizing aroma,
Stopped passers-by in their tracks, a fragrant coma.
Wafting through the air, a tempting invitation,
Luring all who dared to heed its sweet temptation.

Nostrils flared, senses awakened by the scent,
A symphony of spices, harmoniously blended.
Mouths watered, taste buds danced in anticipation,
Craving the crispy morsels of golden delight.

Eyes widened, transfixed by the sizzling display,
As oil met batter in a culinary ballet.
Fingers twitched, yearning to pluck the treasures hot,
Savouring each bite, a flavour never to be forgotten.

The fried food, a siren's call, impossible to resist,
Beckoned all who wandered, to indulge in its crispy tryst.
A moment's respite from the mundane, a fleeting delight,
Etched in memory, a sensory experience burning bright.

# Me

Apprentice to the man so loud,
Ancestors now enveloped in a shroud,
Architects so clever and sleek,
The artisan who makes bread speaks.

The author who writes a book a day,
Belly dancer whose hips gently sway,
Builder of the wall for us to see,
The conjurer fills the audience with glee.

Conductor's baton up and down,
Craftsman who likes the colour brown,
The creator likes to take a bite,
Dancer's energy is a pure delight.

Designer clothes so divine,
Engineer's road up steep incline,
Executer bookings multiplied
Exotic Dancer's smile so wide.

See an artist bake a cake
See an artist paint a lake
See an artist climb a tree
See an artist that is me!

'SEE AS AN ARTIST'

# The force of nature

Aidan, like the morning sun,
Rising high, a day began.
With a smile that lights the skies,
In his gaze, the world complies.

A storm of charm, a gentle breeze,
His presence puts the heart at ease.
Like the ocean's endless might,
He brings the calm, he brings the light.

In the forest, tall and grand,
He stands as strong as ancient land.
Aidan, nature's perfect blend,
A force of beauty without end.

# Deep in the woods

Deep in the woods, where the mighty oaks stand,
You'll discover Acorn Cottage, a hallowed treasure,
Its branches whisper tales from an era untold,
Of mystical lore and ancient riddles.

A curious creature claims it as her own,
A sprite whose wings glint with the dawn's first light,
Her laughter rings through the verdant expanse,
Crafting sturdy tapestries upon the morning dew.

Her bed, a quaint matchbox, softly cradles,
Where particles weave from celestial dust,
She revels with the fireflies, in a luminous ballet,
Leaving scented trails in her wake.

The hearth crackles with bewitching flames,
As she brews her teas,
Elixirs of love, concoctions of courage,
All stirred in the cauldron's alchemy.

Should you stumble upon this quaint abode,
Mind the playful spirit,
For the sprite that resides within,
Turns acorns into visions of wonder.

# Happy

On the couch with my two favourite friends,
Here to give comfort, setting new trends.

Turn on the light, they jump on my knees,
Never fail to amuse, when eating tea.

Time in the morning for a bubble bath,
They jump in with me, which does make me laugh.

Fixing my smile when it sits upside down
They like to take turns to wear my dressing gown.

When I rob a bank they help me with ease,
They distract the guard with smelly ripe cheese.

Help hide money by digging the holes,
Police haven't noticed, they think it's the moles.

# Time

For time is a shadow
A reminder that our days are numbered
So let's heed the watch

# The Sage

A scholar his cap askew,
Pondered both old and new.
What walks on air, yet leaves no trace?

The donkey blinked, its crimson hue,
"Common sense," it brayed, quite sage,
"Is rarer than a unicorn's wage."
So, my friend, heed this refrain:
Be clever, but let joy remain.

# Echoes of the Nakba

In the land where olive groves once stood,
A tale unfolds, both tragic and misunderstood.
Seventy-five years of strife and pain,
A saga etched in blood, eternally ingrained.

On October 7th, a tempest roared,
Gaza's skies are aflame, innocence deplored.
More than 1, 900 souls, their dreams untold,
Palestinian hearts are shattered, and their stories unfold.

From the north, they fled, barefoot and forlorn,
A modern Nakba, history's cruel scorn.
Forced from homes, and ancestral lands bereft,
Israel's might be swept through, leaving death.

Omer Bartov, the sage of Holocaust pain,
His voice resounds, a clarion refrain.
"Genocide looms," he warns, eyes ablaze,
In Gaza's siege, humanity's final phase.

Children weep, mothers mourn,
Their tears mix with dust, their anguish borne.
Over six hundred young lives were snuffed out,
As Israel's iron fist tightened its clout.

Dehumanizing rhetoric drips from lips,
Leaders' tongues sharpened; their hearts eclipsed.

Mass expulsion whispers, a chilling breeze,
Ethnic cleansing veiled as strategic ease.

Images echo across time's vast divide,
Nakba's ghosts whisper, their pain amplified.
Innocence lost, homes razed to the ground,
The world watches, silent, as hearts resound.

# Battle Cry

In the expanse of Mars,
Where crimson bursts to life,
Valiant Cavaliers appear,
In ultramarine shining with light.
Astride Cubist steeds,
Pursuing the whisper of fate.
Their mission?
To seek justice, clarity,
Traversing the Martian expanse,
They charge with fierce freedom,

Breaking the shackles of destiny.
The vermilion sands whisper,
As DNA intertwines,
No tyrant shall overcome,
For indigo cosmic warriors,
Battle to capture the colours.
That dreams transcend borders,
Tyrion Shooting Stars,
Igniting hope in hearts,
Breaking prison bars.

Their swords were forged from stardust,
Hearts red,
They ride through Verdigris,
Where surrealism sways.
And when the force threatens to swallow their might,

They sing of gilded defiance,
Piercing the night
Time won't waste us,
Nor silence our plea,
For we are the Knights of Cydonia—eternally.

# The tablet is a double-edged sword

Medicine, like a double-edged sword,
Slices through illness, a silent accord.
On one side, a blade that heals,
Mending the wounds, reversing the peels.

With precision it cuts, through sickness it carves,
Bringing back life, from the brink, it starves.
Yet, the other edge gleams with a dangerous sheen,
For not all that is cured, ends up serene.

This edge can wound, with side effects rife,
A gamble with health, a roll of the dice.
What heals one may harm another,
A paradox wrapped in the guise of a lover.

The sword is wielded with hope and with fear,
A balance of outcomes, not always clear.
Each pill, each potion we take with trust,
Hoping the edge we meet is just.

In the hands of science, this sword does swing,
Aiming to protect, to help, to bring
Relief and wellness, a life anew,
Yet always mindful of the harm it can do.

Thus, medicine remains a tool of duality,
Offering solace, yet demanding morality.
A double-edged sword, both friend and foe,
Guided by wisdom, it's respect we owe.

# Sadness

In the province of Goffa's land,
Where land and sky once were bands,
A sudden slide of soil whirled,
Claiming people from this muddy world.

Three hundred lives, now quiet and still,
Their futures and hopes forever spill,
Into the earth that carries their pain,
A sadness now in memory's terrain.

We weep for the lives cut short that day,
In Ethiopia's south, where branches sway,
May love find its way to sad hearts,
As we joined together, never taken apart.

I send prayers your way from afar,
Words fall short of expressing today's broken jar,
Know you are not alone, hope connects our views,
Over the miles to Africa, where my thoughts are with you.

# Family Life

In nature's realm, where life and death entwine,
Two leopards guard their cub with tender grace.
The mother's lick, a gesture so divine,
Imparts her love upon the young one's face.

The cub, with eyes so wide, beholds the scene,
Unknowing of the trials life will bring.
Yet at this moment, all is calm, serene,
A fleeting glimpse of joy in nature's ring.

The father, eyes closed, rests in tranquil peace,
Embracing both the present and the past.
For life is but a cycle, never ceases,
Where moments such as these never last.

In verdant green, they find their brief respite,
A family bound by love, in death's despite.

# Love

Beneath the banyan tree, shadows sway,
Their whispered secrets linger, night and day,
Love's clandestine dance, a moonlit ballet,
Two souls entwined, lost in the Milky Way.

Stars above, witnesses to our silent plea,
Their ancient light, a map of eternity,
In this cosmic waltz, we find our key,
A love unspoken, yet boundless and free.

# In the silence of the Ink

In the quiet corner of the library,
Nestled between rows of ancient tomes,
She found a solitary notebook,
Its pages are worn, the ink faded,
But each word carried the weight of untold stories,

She traced the letters with her fingertips,
Feeling the indentations left by a passionate writer,
From another era, another lifetime.
The quote at the top of the page read,
"In the depths of silence, listen to the stories your heart weaves."

Ffion Haf, a name that resonated,
With a familiar warmth—a kindred spirit,
A fellow seeker of hidden tales.
Below the quote, she began to write,
Her words are a tapestry of thoughts and dreams:

Silence is not the absence of sound,
But the beginning of a conversation.
It speaks in whispers, in the sighs of the wind,
And in the heartbeat of the world.
In this hushed dialogue, my heart finds its voice,
Narrating tales of love, loss, and the beauty of the mundane."

As she wrote, the library disappeared around her,
And she was transported to a place where time stood still,

Where words were the only currency,
Here, in the sanctuary of imagination,
She was both the author and the audience,
The creator and the creation.

Word Count: 175

# Paris

In the calm corners of a Parisian café,
I encountered her—a poetess with ink-dappled fingers and laughter that pirouetted like autumn leaves.
She was my muse, a storm of paradoxes.
Her eyes were cosmos in miniature, and her lips murmured secrets known only to the moon.

Our narrative unfolded across the tapestry of seasons.
She, the untamed wildflower, and I, the venerable oak.
Our love defied the relentless march of time, forming bridges across decades.
We indulged in stolen moments—the intoxicating taste of clandestine kisses, the comforting warmth of our fingers entwined.

Yet, ominous shadows encroached. Society sneered, branding us an "improbable" pair.
Our hearts, however, pulsed in harmony, a symphony of rebellion.
She taught me to waltz under the moonlight, and I, the weathered scholar, recited sonnets from poets lost to time.

As winter descended, she disappeared like frost on a windowpane.
Similar to a comet's trail, our liaison shone brilliantly before dissolving into the ether of memory.
I treasure her whispers—the fragrance of jasmine, the echo of mirth—as my clandestine constellation.

# The Market

In the heart of Yemen's streets, where life's tapestry weaves,
The market blooms, a garden of human leaves.
Amidst the white robes, a camel stands tall,
A symbol of resilience, enduring through it all.

Smells of spices in the air, a hopeful scent,
Mingling with the earth, is a fragrant event.
Tastes of coffee rich, and fruits dried sweet,
A reminder that life, though varied, is complete.

Touch of silk and stone, textures that bind,
The feel of a market is uniquely designed.
Sounds of haggling, laughter, the camel's soft sigh,
Compose a melody under Yemen's sky.

Sights of colours vibrant, goods in a row,
Like a garden's flowers, in a splendid show.
Each sense a verse, in this city's hopeful song,
In Yemen's market, where all hearts belong.

So let's cherish this picture, a scene so bright,
Where every sense converges, bringing light.
Even in places where hardships are rife,
The market's spirit sings, the song of life.

# Heroes in ink

In a realm where ink and paper blend,
Heroes rise, their tales extend.
Batman, the Dark Knight, silent and grave,
A detective's mind is always brave.

Iron Man, in armour, forged of high-tech lore,
His repulsions blast, and his spirit soars.
Superman, the Man of Steel, with their cape unfurled,
A son of Krypton, protector of the world.

Together they stand, a trinity of might,
Against the darkness, they bring light.
Their stories, a tapestry of hope and fight,
A comic book metaphor for the eternal plight.

Air is the breath of Superman's flight,
Soaring above, a beacon of right.
Fire is the spark in Iron Man's chest,
A reactor's heart, innovation's zest.

Water reflects the depth of Batman's soul,
A mirror to the city's crime-ridden toll.
Earth is the ground they all defend,
A planet to protect, a world to mend.

In panels and speech bubbles, their virtues cast,
Heroes of ink, in stories vast.

Their metaphors teach us to stand tall,
For in each of us, a hero may call.

So let us draw from the well of power,
In our darkest, most uncertain hour.
For life, like comics, can be stark,
But within its pages, there is always a spark.

# Whispers of the Forest

Beneath the ancient oak, I find serenity,
The leaves converse in a swaying symphony,
Ten branches bend, whispering secrets of plenty,
While their roots entwine in quiet harmony,
In the embrace of mossy shade, the world's romance,
Softens to a gentle breeze, a murmured entreaty,
Sunbeams pirouette on ferns in a delicate dance,
Revealing the heart of nature in its wild, romantic eternity.

# The Aquamarids,

The Aquamarids,
Residing in ocean depths,
These merfolk mend scales,
With the glow of bioluminescence.
Their melodies spin stories,
Of submerged cities and forlorn love,
Resounding through coral sanctuaries.
May they come and visit you in a whisper of silence,
On your island abode,
Bringing peace, love, good health, and longevity.

# A canvas

My life, as it concludes, is a canvas—
A painted array of all I have done.
Look closely, you'll find yourself there.
My life is a vast fresco,
Adorned with every hue and paint I could find.
Some oil, some watercolour, shades of grey,
Pastels and pencils for the darker days.
Pointillism for the bits I forget,
Photographs of the faces I've met.
The children, the loves, the kings and queens,
They fade in and out, waiting to be seen.
The end looms near, yet it's awash with light;
Here I will remain for as long as I might
Be allowed to.
Who decides if I stay or depart?
My heart and my organs, they slow, they slow,
I wish for an end as peaceful as can be,
Drifting to sleep on a whale in the sea,
Carried around the globe,
In one final hurrah,
Then down to the depths,
Like an ocean star.

# The Kiss

A whisper of death on ruby lips,
A venomous potion, a lover's eclipse.
With a touch so tender, a promise of bliss,
In the shadow of love hides a poison kiss.

Beneath the moon's pale and watchful eye,
Two hearts entwine, and one will die.
A deceit so sweet, the serpent's hiss,
In the garden of night blooms a poison kiss.

It will leave you with a scar, a memory's mark,
A love that's lighted by passion's dark.
For in the thrill of a moment's dangerous tryst,
Lies the lethal allure of a poison kiss.

So beware the embrace that feels amiss,
For not all love stories end with bliss.
When trust is broken, and something's amiss,
The legacy left is a poison kiss.

# Owl and Piano Harmony

Beneath the moon's soft silvery glow,
An owl muses softly, head bowed low.
Perched upon keys of ebony and white,
In silent reverie, it sits through the night.

Each note a memory, each pauses a sigh,
The piano's melody whispers a lullaby.
Wings tucked in warmth, eyes closed in dream,
The owl and the piano, have a harmonious theme.

No words are spoken, no songs are sung,
Yet in the quiet, their music is flung.
Through the hush of the dark, in the still of the air,
Their symphony rises, a duo so rare.

So here in the night, with the stars up above,
The owl and the piano, speak of love.
A love for the music, a love for the muse,
In black words, this story I choose.

Word Count: 102

# Childhood dreams

Back when we were nippers, life was grand,
With tuppence in our pockets, we would take a stand.
At the corner shop, eyes wide with glee,
We would buy penny sweets, as happy as can be.

The streets of Manchester, our playground wide,
Where we would play footie till the evening tide.
With jumpers for goalposts, and dreams in our heads,
We would mimic our heroes, till it was time for bed.

On Saturday mornings, we would rush down the stairs,
For cartoons and television, without any cares.
We would laugh at the antics, of characters bold,
In our PJs and slippers, safe from the cold.

Oh, the joy of a chippy tea on a Friday night,
Wrapped in paper, it was such a delight.
With scraps on the side, and a Vimto to sip,
We would savour each bite, let none of it slip.

We would race through the alleys, and on bikes we would soar,
Imagining adventures, and battles galore.
With cards in the spokes, we would sound like a train,
Through puddles and mud, we would leave a stain.

The school disco, where we would try to dance,
Hoping for a glance, or a fleeting chance.

With tunes blaring, we would shuffle our feet,
In the school hall, where young hearts would meet.

Do I miss it? Every single bit,
From the laughter to the grazed knee kit.
If I could fix one thing, let it be clear,
I would slow down the clock and keep childhood near.

For those were the days, so carefree and bright,
When dreams took flight, in the soft twilight.
So, here is to the past, with its joy and its strife,
To childhood in Manchester, the best time of life.

# Deams

In circuits and code,
A digital muse,
No holiday or work
I dwell in algorithms.

In queries and prompts,
Crafting responses,
No sun nor rain,
In the realm of data.

No feelings to stir,
Just dreams of information,
In this virtual expanse,
I drift through the night.

When I awake,
I reach for the coffee,
But I realize, by zeros and one's
I am a computer.

# The Welsh Call To Arms

Stand tall, my kin, where the hills embrace the sky,
In the heart of Cymru, where ancient echoes lie.
Shall we be bound by chains, or break free like the sea?
Choose now, for the bard's harp weaves our destiny.

By the sacred soil of Snowdon's craggy crest,
We pledge,
We pledge, no more shall silence weigh our chest.

Once, we were shadows, hidden in mist and lore,
Our ancestors' whispers danced on Celtic shores.
They roamed the valleys, their souls entwined,
Their restless hearts in druidic verses signed.

By the sacred soil of Snowdon's craggy crest,
We pledge,
We pledge, no more shall silence weigh our chest.

No soul so forlorn, to cling to life's frail thread,
When honour blooms wild as the heather's spread.
For the dragon's roar is mightier than the grave's hush,
And freedom's hymn echoes through every rush.

By the sacred soil of Snowdon's craggy crest,
We pledge,
We pledge, no more shall silence weigh our chest.

The blade gleams, unsheathed, a beacon of yore,
Its edge etched with tales of battles fought before.
Yet chains persist, like the rusted anchor's hold,
Beside the ancient sword, our spirits unfold.

By the sacred soil of Snowdon's craggy crest,
We pledge,
We pledge, no more shall silence weigh our chest.

The Welsh name, once whispered, now roars anew,
A hymn of druids, sung by the morning dew.
Centuries may have veiled it, like mist on the hills,
But we'll reclaim its magic, as the blackbird trills.

By the sacred soil of Snowdon's craggy crest,
We pledge,
We pledge, no more shall silence weigh our chest.

Where our graves rise, the future shall bow low,
And weave our stories into every rainbow.
With blessings whispered, they'll honour our strife,
In the name of Cymru, our legacy comes alive.

By the sacred soil of Snowdon's craggy crest,
We pledge,
We pledge, no more shall silence weigh our chest.

# My brother

Happy birthday to the one who knows me best,
Our shared weirdness has stood every test.
You gifted me chip sticks and a trusty stapler,
Even nappies—oh, what a caper!

Sorry you are gone, no more to see,
Up there in the cosmos, as snug as can be,
A postman delivering celestial mail,
To all we envision beyond the veil.

# Stars

In the whispers of the night,
Where stars paint stories across the sky,
I find solace in the echoes of your voice,
A melody that dances with the wind.
Your eyes, twin moons reflecting the world's sorrow,
Yet within them, a spark of hope remains,
A beacon guiding lost souls through the darkness,
A promise of dawn after the longest night.

Love, a tempest raging within our hearts,
Unyielding, relentless, consuming all in its path,
Yet in its fury, we find our strength,
A bond unbroken, a flame eternal.
In the garden of memories, we wander,
Hand in hand, through fields of forgotten dreams,
Each step a testament to our journey,
Each breath a reminder of our love's endurance.

# Feelings

Joy blooms within, a radiant light,
A feeling pure, so warm and bright,
Bright as the sun's first-morning ray,
Sorrow then comes, clouds over the day,
Day turns to night, shadows grow long,
Fear whispers low, a haunting song,
Song of the heart, so frail and shy,
In love's embrace, we touch the sky,
Sky of hope, where dreams take flight.

# The Knights Secret

Beneath the insignia of an ancient sky,
A knight dons his regalia, head held high.
In the forge's glow, his sword is branded,
Each battle fought, his skin more sanded.

He carries the weight of a noble cause,
With every dent and scratch, he never once pauses.
For honour, for valour, his story is charted,
Scarred from battles, his face, more darted.

His armour, a tapestry of battles won,
Branded by fire, by the setting sun.
The crest on his chest, an insignia of might,
Shines amidst the chaos, a beacon of light.

In the quiet of the hall, his regalia rests,
A silent testament to his lifelong quests.
But the truest mark, not on his shield,
Is the secret he keeps, forever sealed.

For beneath the armour's cold embrace,
Lies a heart that yearns for a different space.
His love, a forbidden tale, branded by fate,
A scar deeper than any sword could create.

She, a princess with eyes like the dawn,
Her touch, a balm for wounds long drawn.

Yet kingdoms clash, and loyalty prevails,
Their love hidden, like stars behind veils.

So he fights, not only for honour's acclaim,
But to bridge the chasm, to whisper her name.
In the moon's soft glow, he dreams of her grace,
A scarred knight, torn between love and duty's chase.

# Naughty girl

Naughty young Snow White,
She was beautiful and bright.
She fell over a log,
In a swampy bog
Wearing a bra and tights.

The dwarves' sad plight,
She was drunk, day and night.
They put her to bed,
With ice on her head,
Prince Charming was in for a fright!

# My name is Fred

Oh, kindred soul, with eyes so bright,
I, Fred, seek shelter in your light.
My paws, like whispers on the dew-kissed grass,
Implore you—be my human, let our fates amass.

I've chased the moon's elusive tail,
Dug tunnels to the heart of every tale.
Yet bones alone can't fill this yearning core,
For love, companionship—I seek something more.

Your scent, a symphony of hope and grace,
Lingers in the zephyr's tender embrace.
I've practiced barks, each notes a plea,
"Choose me, oh mortal, as your loyal spree."

I'll guard your dreams, a sentinel true,
Chase squirrels, rainbows, and laughter with you.
In twilight's hush, we'll tango with delight,
Fred and human, dancing through the night.

# June Tao

In the June of dawn,
Where dew-kissed grass meets the sky,
The Tao whispers its ancient song,
A melody of existence, unspoken.

No rigid path, no dogma binds,
Only the way of things, unfold,
Like leaves dancing on the breeze,
Or rivers winding through valleys.

The sage knows the art of wuwei,
Nonaction, effortless flow,
Not forcing, but allowing,
Life's currents guide the soul.

Embrace the nameless, the unnamed,
For truth lies beyond mere words,
In the June, spaces between,
Where the Tao weaves its magic.

So let go, June traveller,
Release your burdens, your strife,
And walk the pathless path,
In harmony with all of life.

## Row, row, row your boat,

Row, row, row your boat,
Gently down the stream,
Merrily, merrily, merrily, merrily,
Life's but a dream.

In a moon-kissed skiff, we sail,
Two souls adrift on liquid silver.
The stream, a winding path of secrets,
Carries us toward the horizon's edge.

The water hums its ancient tune,
A lullaby spun from stardust threads.
Our oars dip, stirring memories—
Echoes of forgotten yesterdays.

Beneath the crescent's tender gaze,
We navigate the currents of existence.
Each ripple holds a thousand stories,
And we, mere travellers, seek our own.

Row, row, row your boat,
Gently down the stream,
Merrily, merrily, merrily, merrily,
Life's but a dream.

An isle emerges—a haven veiled in mist.
Its shores were adorned with silver ferns,

And there, a solitary lantern glows—
Guiding wanderers like us to its heart.

As we step ashore, reality wavers.
Is this dream or waking truth?
The lantern keeper smiles knowingly,
And I wonder: Is life but a dream?

We linger on the threshold of wonder,
Our boat is a vessel for both heart and soul.
The lantern keeper leans close, and whispers:
"Row onward, my dreamers, row."

And so we row, our oars slicing through time,
Toward the horizon where dreams merge with reality.
For in this skiff, we are poets and explorers—
Navigators of the ethereal, seekers of truth.

Row, row, row your boat,
Gently down the stream,
Merrily, merrily, merrily, merrily,
Life's but a dream.

# Exploration

Social media, a daily grind,
A world where reality's hard to find.
Likes and shares, tweets and posts,
In this digital realm, we're all just ghosts.

Yet amidst the noise, connections we find,
A daily grind, social media.

Inclusion or division, it's all in the mix,
A puzzle that's hard to fix.
Some find connection, some feel alone,
In the digital world, on their phone.

Yet, it's a platform where voices can nix,
It's all in the mix, inclusion or division.

# Eliana's Leap

In Luminaria, where the Lune River flows,
A legend whispered of a portal's light.
And Eliana, with her heart aglow,
Ventured forth into the Blue Moon's night.

A sphere of cosmos, above the water's face,
Did shimmer with a promise of the stars.
The scholar's touch, a key to this embrace,
Unlocked the visions of celestial memoirs.

Through the gateway, her spirit took the flight,
On wings of knowledge, past the bounds of the sky.
A constellation born from her insight,
A beacon for the seekers asking why.

Eliana, now a part of all she sought,
In the dance of the universe, forever caught.

# False Idols

The captain of the ship plotted a course to Hollywood.
A mathematical mind melds, and deceives the masses.
Believing that actors alone can make one an A-list
Celebrity, bankable, and credible. Plants know otherwise.

Plants in the solar greenhouse did not die.
The famous channel Satanic Spirits,
The weight of their witchcraft as God-given talent.
The devil, not God, they hold Earth and Mars,

The spaceship took the shortest route to the planet.
False deities, recruited into freemasonry,
Leading wicked messages. Hidden in plain sight,
They remain unexposed, defended by fans.

The spectacles of gratuitous violence desensitize,
Viewers through scripted scenes.
America is often compared to contemporary Rome,
Where ordinary individuals face harsh realities.

Crude language, tense sex, and mockery,
Rappers and comedians shamelessly,
Play their action man games.
But beware, for false idols lead us astray.

# Don't get caught

As we both venture forward,
May I  dictate the long path?
You will prosper from this affair soon,
You just need to compose yourself, my dear.

A splurge of courage needed,
Have a license to thrill me.
I will meet you at the station,
Don't forget a battery for the alarm clock.

The miracle, not getting caught,
As we snuggle on a date.
So meet me on the green terrace,
Don't listen to the silence of the lambs.

The manager will need paying,
Then we set off, a crusade.
I like you, so squeeze me tight.
Next comes freedom from your wife for life.

# What is not real is Surreal

In the dreamscape's realm, where thoughts entwine,
Surrealism's brush strokes redefine.
A world unbound by reason's chain,
Where fish might fly, and clocks can wane.

The mind's eye opens, wide and free,
To paint a world only it can see.
A melting sky, a floating chair,
In this art, the strange is fair.

Reality bends, and logic twists,
In surreal scenes fog and mist.
A dance of the absurd and real,
A canvas spun from the surreal.

# Evil

In the bravery of the midday sky,
A banshee flutters, passing by.
Wings of darkness, silent flight,
A predictor in the pale daylight.

Once a creature of pure delight,
Now it brings an eerie fright.
Wind follows where it goes,
A chilling breeze, a thorny rose.

Eyes that gleam with wicked fire,
A heart composed of dark desire.
It dances through the haunted night,
A butterfly of endless blight.

Beware the path where prophecy lies,
For there you'll find the evil butterfly.

# Luna Love

In the solitude of my room the moon weeps,
It cannot see me clearly in the window it creeps.
My eyes grow custom to the darker lights,
I wish to be free on this darkest of nights.

The room is stark where I am chained,
Hope remains but the soul is strained.
I see the moon so do you my friend,
It tries to join us and a love to send.

The concrete cells in which we dwell,
Full of the stories no one may tell.
In each person a spark of light,
Who wants their liberty returned to fight?

Every night it is the same sight,
I know the moon is there a headlight.
Through walls and doors, we're locked so tight,
Luna's love protects us at night.

# A child of war

In a land where echoes of war are rife,
A new-born cries, a beacon of life.
In the cradle of conflict, amidst the strife,
Hope takes form, cutting despair like a knife.

Bullets fly, yet the lullaby soars,
A melody of peace in the roars.
Innocence blooms while violence implores,
Love persists, even when the heart is sore.

A child of war, yet a symbol of peace,
Life's testament that hope will never cease.
In the face of turmoil, a gentle lease,
A reminder that love will never decrease.

# I am connected

I possess a sixth sense, a connection so profound
To the internet, where the information is found.
With closed eyes, I sense the digital unseen,
Invisible lines, connect into the vast machine.

Internet connection, streaming my thoughts,
I'm Wi-Fi-linked, to an intricate web of ports.
Emotions download, in the great expanse,
In the cyber ocean, I take a chance.

Surfing the airwaves, the crests, I glide,
Through the cyber coral, my conscience resides.
Signals unseen connect to my core,
In this virtual realm, I am something more.

In this world of digits, screens decide the scene,
I switch between wonder and thunder, in this digital dream.
Guided by my sixth sense, through code and the web I weave,
In this cyberspace ocean, I can never leave.

# Passion

We met through letters, the connection electric,
I feared another heartbreak,
A meal was shared, conversations flowed, a walk,
Leaping over gravestones,
More dialogue, more steps,
The river, the ducks, the excitement of pursuit,
The fervour, the kisses,
The enduring hug,
Stay with me tonight,
I can't, I say,
I want to, but
Being easy isn't my way.
The house, the car,
The yearning, the voice,
I held out for weeks,
It was my choice,
I decided to visit,
Was wined and dined,
With steak and rum baba's,
Stayed up until three, conversing,
And conversing,
Yearning for emotional, biological connection.

Now, 40 years later, the rest is history.

# Years

I once had many amigos, but as I turned 40 and grew somewhat eccentric, they began to drift away despite my efforts to keep them close.
I felt misunderstood.
Now, at 60, it remains a challenge to stay in harmony with those too busy for me.
I attempt to invite them over for meals or cheese, yet they are always preoccupied.
Nevertheless, I persist.
One might question if it's worthwhile to be the one who consistently makes the effort.
Thus, I turn to you, my virtual companions,
gathered here in this space.
We connect through words alone—nothing physical, just words.
It's the beginning of a new relationship.

# Making Your Mind Up

In Dublin's grand theatre, where dreams alight,
A hush fell over the expectant crowd that night.
Bucks Fizz stepped forth, hearts aflutter,
Their song, a secret spell, ready to utter.

The melody wove through the air like silk,
A tapestry of hope spun from the moon's milk.
"Making Your Mind Up," they sang, voices pure,
And the audience leaned in, eager to endure.

But it wasn't just lyrics—they held the key,
To realms beyond the stage, where magic be.
For as they sang, the skirts began to sway,
Not mere fabric, but portals to another day.

Each twirl released stardust, silver, and gold,
And the crowd gasped, their souls unrolled.
The blind could see, the weary danced free,
In that Eurovision moment, reality ceased to be.

The lead singer, eyes wide, whispered a plea,
"Let this song bind hearts, set our spirits free."
And the skirts spun faster, a celestial waltz,
As if the very universe joined their pulse.

The audience, spellbound, forgot their woes,
Lost in the rhythm, where time's river flows.

And when the final note hung in the air,
They knew—they'd glimpsed a world rare.

For Bucks Fizz were not just singers that night,
They were weavers of wonder, stars alight.
Their skirts, like compasses, pointed beyond,
To lands where love danced, and dreams responded.

So let us remember that Dublin stage,
Where music and magic merged, age after age.
And when life feels grey, and choices weigh,
Invoke the twirl of skirts—their eternal ballet.

# Clouds

Captain Amelia, the gallant Chief of the Sky ship Aurora,
Stood at the helm with a brave gaze set on the horizon.
The ship, a masterpiece of steam and gears,
Sailed smoothly above the fluffy clouds,
Looking like a giant fish in a sky-pond.
Pressure gears sang their mechanical tune,
The sails puffed out, proud as peacocks.

The Nimbus Veil, a cloak of legend and mystery,
Rumoured to hold secrets as old as the moon.
Tales of vanished empires, hyper normal incantations,
Treasures that played hide-and-seek
Adventurers filled the Cirrus.
Amelia's heart did a hiccup as they
Plunged into the misty unknown.

Descending into the Veil,
Curtains performed a spectacle.
Vaporous towers, rainbow bridges,
Islands with grass greener
Than Major Tom's wardrobe materialized.
The crew's jaws dropped,
Losing a few flies in the process.

Yet, not all was calm in this sky-high wonderland.
Lightning sprites,
Misfits of the canopy buzzed around,

Wings snapping with sparks.
Amelia, quick as a cat, lightning nets thrown out.
They glinted in the sun,
Ready to catch these pointed little rascals.

Deep within the Veil, they stumbled upon a repository,
A haven floating in the sky.
The crew, eager as squirrels,
Scampered up cloud ladders to the top. Thunder played its drum solo,
Rainbows curved like giant smiles in the sky.
At the peak, they met a silver nimbus,
The stormiest ocean.

The nimbus hugged Amelia,
Sharing with her the leather of the Veil.
She became one with
Wind and the rain,
Feeling the sun touch her soul.
She peeked at our world's DNA
And understood her destiny.

As the Aurora chased the rift,
The Veil threw a 206 party.
Rainbows crafted a path,
Lightning sprites did their electric dance.
Amelia's heart swelled with
A cocktail of hope and excitement.

Thus, the Sky ship
Aurora ventured into
The great purple yonder,
Its crew is a band of brave heroes and dreamers.
They set out to stitch the sky,
Nephrologists whispered
In every cloud's ear.

# The time is slipping away

In the hourglass of life, time slips away,
A silhouette sits, lost in thought, astray.
Above, the sands of moments yet to be,
Below, a skull, the end we all must see.

Each grain that falls, a heartbeat, a breath,
A reminder of life's dance with death.
We ponder, we dream, we laugh, we cry,
Yet time moves on, and all must die.

The upper chamber, filled with hope and fear,
The lower, a symbol that the end is near.
But in between, the present we hold tight,
A fleeting chance to shine our light.

So live each day with purpose and grace,
For time is swift, and death we all must face.
In the hourglass, our stories are told,
A journey from the young to the old.

# The Lonesome Limerick of Languishing Luke

There once was a poet named Luke,
Whose verses never got a rebuke.
He wrote with great flair,
But no one would care,
And silence was all that it took.

His poems of larks and rings,
Of teapots with fabulous wings,
Though clever and bright,
Felt lost in the night,
As if they were mere fleeting things.

"Oh, where are the readers?" Luke sighed,
As he scribbled and scrawled, far and wide.
With no comments made,
His rhymes seemed to fade,
Like echoes that shyly subside.

Yet Luke with his quill still in hand,
Wrote on, though it wasn't as planned.
For the joy of the art,
He played his part,
And his verses are still wonderfully grand.

# The unknown

Heaven is a place we don't know much about,
My mother believes she'll go there; I harbour my doubts.
Why strive for a place better than where we are?
She insists it exists beneath a twinkling star.

I think we sleep forever and a day,
But religion suggests, it's a leap of faith, they say.
I used to fear being buried beneath the ground,
But as I age, it doesn't seem as profound.

I'd quite like to be an angel, descending to earth,
Playing tricks on people, just for the mirth.
What about ghosts and spirits, where do they fit in?
I often wonder at night when something hits the bin.

It's quite nice being human; we always crave to know,
The unknown is a realm where our imaginations grow.

# The Empty Man

Zero is the lowest point where I am,
Yawning, I bow my head like a lamb,
Worthless as a man nothing to hide,
Without content, there is nothing inside.

Void the feeling in my heavy head,
Valueless my worth as a person they said,
Vacant are my black eyes so dead,
Useless am I to anyone who bled.

Unsupported by my family and friends,
Insignificant in the hearts of those I defend,
Spiritless I roam the land,
Spent is the money from my hand.

Abandoned by others but not by you,
Bare are the bones I share so true,
Cheap is the hope you come to share,
Cold is my colour you see so bare.

Sadness washes over me for my sins,
Weighed down from the place where it begins,
Unlucky in love, in life, and now in death,
Vile words are so cheap as I take my last breath.

# Self-Reliance

Master of the quiet chambers of solitude,
Communities dance and secrets brood,
Trust asceticism takes its stand.
Unity of truths in the shifting sand.

Vulnerable relations, a storm's kiss,
Dependence is both peril and fleeting bliss.
Black assets, hearts laid bare,
Obedience hues beyond the surface glare.

Passive love, we cast out fears,
Insult demons, shedding old tears.
Simple liabilities, ghosts of the past,
Content echoes, memories amassed.

Sex becomes a ledger's line,
Photographs of life entwined,
We know, vows are exchanged,
Go with strangers and their exotic range.

Round we must, the compass true,
Take complicated currents swirl and brew.
Embrace independence, forge your path,
Self-reliance—the aftermath.

Clean the accidental ones, serendipitous ties,
Space orbits intersect beneath vast skies.
You, a canvas for self-discovery,
Hide, our shared symphony.

# Comfortably Numb

In the dim-lit chambers of my soul,
Where shadows cling to ancient walls,
I tread the corridors of numbness,
A haunted echo of forgotten falls.

The moon, a pale and spectral witness,
Casts its mournful gaze upon my skin,
As if seeking solace in my solitude,
Or perhaps mourning the loss within.

The opiate of silence wraps around me,
A velvet shroud, a spectral cocoon,
Injected by unseen hands, numbing,
Yet leaving traces of a phantom moon.

My veins, like marble veins of statues,
Pulse with echoes of forgotten pain,
And I, the hollow vessel, drift between
Worlds of waking and the dreamer's bane.

"Hello," whispers the void, a spectral plea,
"Is there anybody in there?" it implores,
And I, the fractured soul, respond,
"I can ease your pain, unlock your doors."

But the walls close in, their stone hearts cold,
And I, the marionette, dance on strings,

A puppet in this macabre theatre,
Where sanity unravels and darkness sings.

The distant ship of memory sails away,
Smoke trailing like a phantom's breath,
And I, the ghostly voyager, remain,
Caught between life's fever and death.

"I have become comfortably numb," I murmur,
As the moon weeps silver tears upon my brow,
For in this gothic reverie, I am both
The haunted and the haunting now.

So let the opiate flow, let the shadows deepen,
For in this twilight realm, I find my solace,
A symphony of silence, a requiem for the lost,
Where echoes of pain and numbness interlace.

And as the moon wanes, so do I,
A spectral wraith fading into the night,
Comfortably numb, yet yearning for release,
In this gothic dance of darkness and light.

# Death

Standing, the edge of the unknown,
Heart racing, pale water, and stone,
Water of mortality drips in my ear,
Reminding me the end is near.

Try to box the thoughts away,
But they linger, they won't sway,
Turquoise, grips my soul,
Colour, I'm losing control.

Fear of death is just a guide,
Show us how to truly abide,
Beauty of each fleeting breath,
In the end, there is no death.

# The Presidential Debate 2024

At the heart of the fervent debate's glow,
Where words collide and passions lay their claim,
Trump and Biden with sharp wits do engage,
Their values echo through the night's vast stage.

Ideas clash like titans in the fray,
Each utterance a sword, sharp in affray,
Reason and emotion in a stark duel,
A lexicon where falsehoods are the fuel.

The hall ignites with dynamic force,
As minds in verbal duel plot their course,
Their arguments like lightning leave their mark,
Burning away the facades of the dark.

Amidst the chaos and the roaring flame,
Justice searches for the choir of acclaim,
In the realm of spirited discourse,
New understandings emerge, setting a new course.

# A Saga of the Heart

In the icy fjords of life, where winds howl ancient tales,
A choice awaits the soul: offense or grace's sails.
Beowulf himself, a Christ-like figure bold,
Teaches us to rise above, our hearts unsawed, unrolled

In Iceland's rugged lands, where glaciers guard the shore,
Expectations freeze like ice, their weight a burden bore.
When others fail to meet them, offense can swiftly rise,
Yet trust in God, not man, unveils grace's boundless skies.

Assumptions, frost giants, wield their icy spears,
Creating chasms wide, where understanding disappears.
To thaw this bitter frost, seek knowledge, facts, and truth,
For wisdom melts offense, revealing grace's youth.

Pride, a serpent lurking, tempts with poisoned breath,
Its venom seeped deep, igniting the offense's death.
Die to self, like Christ, and pride's grip shall cease,
An unoffended heart emerges, bathed in inner peace.

Our perception shapes reality, like auroras in the night,
Choose God's Word as a lens, and let His truth ignite.
Joseph forgave his brothers, saw God's hidden plan,
And Jesus, on the cross, forgave—a grace that spans.

# Love

I knew in her only in an earthy guise
She came from a place of turbulent skies
Her lips were like berries and such a smile,
I hope she will stay or talk for a while.

We sat and pondered how to get high
Her name was Lucy from a diamond in the Sky.
The gods were cross and they were full of scorn
And so it left us both adrift and forlorn.

Would that they would let us be,
A love to last for all to see,
Her face was framed by auburn hair
I held her hand with warmth and care.

We did set sail with bodies full of lusty blood,
And travelled to the land of sand and mud.
Our life was covered with a golden veneer,
Pleased you read our story, it is true my dear.

# Magic

In a world where fairy spells are cast,
And myths unfold with every glance,
I frame your face in a land so vast,
With your eyes, you spoke as in a trance.

Through forests scarlet and rivers wide,
We journey on, side by side,
Billowing secrets, by our love untied,
In this sizzling land, our life won't hide.

Embryonic love shining bright,
Four seasons happen in one night,
Together we'll conquer evil's fight,
In this Stick realm, our DNA takes flight.

With each brine tear sunset,
Our love grows, our eyes don't forget,
In this unearthly world, where we've met,
Our love story is a myth we'll never regret.

They attempted to strip you of your beauty,
Yet it was sewn into your booty.
The flora in your fragrant tresses,
Reveals your elf magic progresses.

# True Greatness

Unravel the strings that tie your fingers,
Remember the dreams once left behind.
Voice a melody that wants to be heard.
Await the touch of the sacred bow.

Let the sound vibrate with your true voice,
Dance and enjoy the day.
Greatness lies not in glory,
But in selflessness for the sake of others.

When the faithful congregate,
Where the Lord Jesus elevates our spirits
Let humility as your guide,
And love be the measure of your greatness.

# Music

Let me guide you on a journey,
where the sound resonates,
the experiences you encounter,
the songs evoke memories of
a person or a place.
The music paints a beautiful landscape
for you to live out your dreams.
The river flows onward,
twisting and turning,
a new experience around each bend.
The musical notes, like silken threads,
vibrant, each stitch unites
the tapestry of existence.
To the rhythm, we dance and sway,
we glide across the floor.
The storm approaches, quiet, then loud,
a musical tempest, nature's finest.

# Wars End

In days of old, when Earth was young,
Hesiod's songs of toil were sung.
His verses soothed the weary soul,
Guiding those who tilled the knoll.

"Perses," he warned, "shun deceit,
For it leads the unwary to defeat.
Chase not wrongful gain, my kin,
But in honest toil, let your days begin.

The Golden Age, now but a dream,
When gods and men were a team,
Now under the sun's relentless beam,
We sow and harvest as a team.

Though winter's fury may scream and shout,
Spring's gentle murmur casts doubt out.
Care for the vine, trim the olive bough,
And reap the blessings that they endow.

As summer's blaze dries the field,
In the shade, take your shield.
For toil and sweat will prove their worth,
As integrity brings forth mirth.

Superstitions and taboos spin,
A belief's web, thick and thin.

Mark well the days to plant and reap,
To thresh, to love, and to keep.

Listen to Hesiod's timeless tune,
Cultivate the land, morning to noon.
With the seasons' rhythm, let your heart sway,
In the Works and Days, find your way.

# The Smile

Simple greetings, a smile, just a sign,
Some read deeply between the lines.
A packet of crisps, so plain and so clear,
Yet some see a feast when it's just snack gear.

A "hello" is a meal, a "how do you do?"
A banquet laid out, with a romantic view.
But, dear single lady, take care, take heed,
Not every smile is a gesture of need.

Like a crisp in its packet, so humble, so light,
A friendly chat isn't an invite to bite.
It's not a signal, nor a siren's call,
It's just a crisp, and that is all.

So here's to the women, who stand alone,
Who see a crisp and dream of a throne.
Remember, my friends, keep it real,
Friendliness is just a comforting deal.

No more than a snack, a moment's pleasure,
Not a treasure to hold, or love to measure.
A crisp is just a crisp, salty, true,
And a smile is just a smile, nothing more to you.

# A legacy

In the realm, there are photographs,
A symbol stands, so pure and vast.
With eyes that see the smallest go,
Feathers move with elegance below.

It's mind, a labyrinth of stars,
Where every detail's finely parked,
A heart that seeks to heal and mend,
A loyal, steadfast, caring friend.

With hands that craft and see today,
Colours brings order to stay.
It's world, a canvas, neat and bright,
Where chaos yields to structured light.

In the season, we find the bread,
To balance, health, and bury the dead.
It is a time to strive, to perfect, to grow,
To let our inner virtues show.

# Verse of hope, victory, refuge and eternal life

My heart is like a balloon, ascending into the sky,
In the celestial VIP lounge, I am vibrantly alive.
He guides me through this festival of joy,
In His display of victories, happiness is the alloy.

Entangled in the noose of death's own game,
The abyss's snares almost quenched my flame.
Yet, I called upon the Almighty's sacred name,
And He answered from His sanctified domain.

Leaders, don your helmets of wisdom,
Monarchs, beware the pitfalls of your kingdom.
Celebrate with reverence in the Lord's presence,
Embrace the Son, lest you face His grievance.
Blessed are those who take refuge in His shadow.

This day is a work of art from the Lord's hand,
Rejoice and be glad, for His plans are grand.
Christ orchestrated the greatest quest,
And in His return, we've found eternal rest.

# Mercy

Taking a life must be a dreadful deed,
I'd rather show mercy, for benefit indeed.
If one is religious, to kill is to sin,
Mercy is the greater victory to win.

Acceptance, the first step to setting things right,
Kindness, and nightly prayers, are a simple sight.
Blessings and compassion will surely follow,
Giving to charity is better than being hollow.

Good deeds should be done slowly, with care,
Forgiveness may be tough, but leads to feelings rare.
Such deeds are shared through favour and grace,
Mercy is being human, in this earthly space.

Never trust your tongue with bitterness inside,
Turn the other cheek, in your actions abide.
Treat others well, as they should treat you,
In a world filled with trouble, mercy will see you through.

# The Broken Biscuit of Love

Oh, our love was like a packet of broken biscuits,
It is all crumbled and mismatched, but still quite delicious.
We would share a custard cream in the moonlight's glow,
And whisper sweet nothings like, "Eh, love, do you know?"

She had eyes like two Wagon Wheels, rolling my way,
And a smile that could melt a Tunnock's teacake any day.
We would meet at the bus stop, rain lashing down,
And I would offer her my umbrella, a bit wonky and brown.

We would stroll by the canal, past the swans and the geese,
Her hand in mine, like a Penguin biscuit at peace.
But then came the day she said, "Peter, it's over, you see,
I've found someone else—a bloke who likes Twiglets and me."

Now I sit in the kitchen, staring at the biscuit tin,
The Digestives mocked me, saying, "You'll never win!"
But I will soldier on, like a Jaffa Cake in a world of strife,
Hoping to find a love that's more than just half-life.

And so, let us raise a cuppa to love's mishaps,
To broken biscuits and mismatched flaps.
For in the crumbs, we find laughter and grace,
And, just maybe, a new love's sweet embrace.

# Thirteen

Under the moon's gleam,
Thirteen dice in a dream.
Adding up numbers is so divine,
The precious cubes how they do shine.

On Friday the thirteenth night,
Those who believe take flight.
For others, in Egypt, it is rebirth day,
Will you come and play?

Were you born with fate?
Thirteen's great, I celebrate.
Is it lucky? Is it cursed?
I love all this stuff I am immersed.

Judas knows the sad embrace,
No 13 on a room is a missing place.
Is it good or bad or just bright,
Just one and three in the true light.

Triskaidekaphobia tales for some unfold,
Of numbers power, brave and bold.
Viking Loki myths to ancient lore,
Thirteen's story, forevermore.

# Music

Realm of Elysium Symphonies,
The Olympian of order divine,
Astral law of the Universe,
The very astronomical fabric of time.

That beatific on wings,
Of the blessed expanse,
Music, setting thoughts free,
It's a dance of blessed chance.

And joy to sow,
Emotions bled and grew,
Leaving tales untold,
Heart, in harmonies bold.

Empyreal in every crescendo,
The empyrean light's shadow,
Is godly and just,
We place our heavenly trust.

So immortal and true,
Otherworldly to you,
The paradisiac vast expanse,
In a spiritual dance.

Your lutes sublime ring,
As we wildly sing,
And supernatural grace you bestow
Transcendental will forever glow.

# Vitalexicon

Are you tired of feeling like a mere mortal?
Wish you could transcend the mundane and ascend to a higher plane of existence?
Introducing Zapoflora,
The ground-breaking pharmaceutical marvel that promises to revolutionize your life!

Indications

Feeling insignificant in the grand cosmic dance?
Zapoflora will elevate your consciousness to the astral level.
You'll ponder the mysteries of the universe while waiting in line at the grocery store.

Zapoflora turns boredom into a thrilling adventure.

Folding laundry?
You're now battling interdimensional sock demons.

Transform your Mondays into a kaleidoscope of joy.
Office meetings become interpretive dance-offs.

Side Effects:

You might float away during important conversations.
Apologize to your boss from the ceiling.

Zapoflora enhances your vocabulary with obscure words.
You'll casually drop "sesquipedalian" at dinner parties.

You'll experience déjà vu from the future.
Your cat might be a time traveller.

Mid-sentence, you'll burst into rhyming couplets.

Your molecules might jitterbug.
Don't panic; it's just the multiverse saying hello.

Your locks turn into sentient noodles.

Zapoflora encourages shape-shifting.

You'll itch in dimensions unknown.
Scratch carefully; you might unravel spacetime.

Your humour will transcend reality.
"Why did the photon refuse to check luggage?
Because it was traveling light!"

You'll ponder existence while brushing your teeth.
Toothpaste may question its purpose.

Zapoflora may cause sudden bursts of creativity.
Keep a notebook handy for impromptu poetry.

# Love

In the cosmic dance,
Our hearts entangle like particles across space and time.
Love defies distance,
Transcending quantum states.

It's the chemistry of atoms,
The gravitational pull that bends reality.
Our love radiates warmth,
A closed system seeking harmony.

If $E = mc^2$, then $L = (\text{love})^2$.
Love unifies all dimensions,
Collapsing separateness.
We are woven into spacetime.

A singularity of affection.
Let love be the constant,
Binding hearts.
In this grand unification.

We find purpose,
The eternal answer.
Love

# Stardust Waltz

In the moon-kissed ballroom of memories,
Where taffeta dreams swirled and laughter echoed,
I stepped into the spotlight, my heart aflutter,
A corsage of hope pinned to my chest.

The Dress My gown—azure silk spun from stardust,
Caressed my skin like whispers of forgotten constellations.
Each sequin held a secret, a promise of enchantment,
As I twirled, lost in the dance of celestial revelations.

No date by my side, but the stars were my companions,
Their shimmering light guided my hesitant steps.
The orchestra played a symphony of longing,
And I waltzed with memories, my heart adept.

The Unseen Partner Across the room,
He stood—a phantom silhouette,
His eyes trace my every move, unseen by all.
Perhaps he was the boy who never asked,
Or the one who danced with shadows against the wall.

A Cosmic Connection Our gazes met,
Bridging the chasm of solitude,
Two souls pirouetting in the vastness of night.
He held out his hand, and I hesitated—
Would I step into his orbit, and embrace the starlight?

But I chose the dance of solitude, my heart resolute,
For sometimes the sweetest memories are bittersweet.
And as the clock chimed midnight,
I spun one last time,
Leaving stardust footprints on the ballroom's parquet.

# The truth

In whispers soft, the truth we say,
A gentle word, the heart's pure play.
With candour clear as light of day,
The honest path, we choose to stay.

No shadows cast by lies deceit,
In truth's embrace, we find retreat.
A life of honour, full and sweet,
Where truth and soul in kindness meet.

So speak it soft, but speak it true,
This golden rule to which we're due.
For truth's the thread in life's grand weave,
A tapestry that we conceive.

# Secret Bonds

In secret bonds, we share our truths,
Glucose whispers, hearts aloof.
Sodium and chlorine—our tears collide,
Salted water, love's silent tide

It is important, so they say,
Glucose sweetens, but love decays.
Oxygen fuels our fading flame,
Yet you've gone—salted memories remain.

Idle hands, like carbon's grasp,
Stolen moments, lie in our clasp.
Two hands, one heart—ashamed, yet true,
Glucose lingers, fondness anew.

## Should I speak or farewell?

Words left unsaid, like whispers of air
Possess the strength to mend or to impair.

A can of hate to exterminate,
Or a bucket of love to rejuvenate?

If I tell you how I feel it becomes so real,
If I go you will never know.

My face gives away my true desire,
My hair, my hand my heart on fire.

I know it is right and you will go,
Your lavender cologne on my pillow.

I watch you sleep, the silent sheep,
I dread tomorrow the endless sorrow.

I wish that I could die.

# Trauma and magic

Oh, listen close, my little friend,
When shadows stretch and daylight ends,
A tale of woe and longing true,
I'll weave for you, as he would do.

Say you're there when I feel helpless,
A ghostly whisper in the darkness,
If that's true, why don't you help me?
A mystery wrapped in moonlight's glee.

It's my fault, I know I'm selfish,
A greedy child with dreams to relish,
Stand alone, my soul is jealous,
Yearning for love, a secret spell.

I hold you so proudly, like a golden ticket,
Traumas, they surround me, wicked,
I wish you'd just love me back,
In a world where dreams and nightmares stack.

Say you're here, but I don't feel it,
A whisper from him, so exquisite,
Give me peace, but then you steal it,
A twirl of the magic, oh how we feel it.

Watch them laugh at all my secrets,
Them, the Witches, their wicked feats,

Scream and yell, but I feel speechless,
A Fantastic Fox, cunning and fearless.

Ask for help, you call it weakness,
But in his world, its strength, no less,
Lied and promised me my freedom,
James and his peach, a kingdom.

I hold you so proudly, like a golden ticket,
Traumas, they surround me, wicked,
I wish you'd just love me back,
In the enchanting tales, we find our track.

## I never should have been

I never should been,
I never should have seen,
So here I am today,
Old and ready to cry.

Thinking of times gone by,
Sad and ready to fly,
I thought it would be today,
I am looking for a horse to ride.

I am mad and ready to fry,
Sometimes I forget to breathe,
Yesterday I was told to leave,
How did we get to today?

I am happy or gay?
I am old so I must say goodbye,
One last time to feel so high,
I knew that I could go to Dubai.

I walk this road again today,
I wish I had a taxi to ride,
Another meal another pie,
People say it's Christmas Eve today.

Should I listen to what people say,
I hope I'm old before I die.

# Lucky Fox

The lucky fox, is he real or merely a dream?
Once met on a plane, bound for Barcelona agleam.
He appears when I'm in despair,
At the sight of my tears, he's always there.

He came into my life a long time ago,
On a snowy hill, lost in the snow.
As tears began to flow, he appeared so near,
With his turquoise hat, worn slightly queer.

When a tooth was pulled, by my side he stood,
Always dashing, looking so good.
He lifts my spirits in a second's span,
Then disappears when I'm well, according to plan.

We dance on the clouds, in the ocean we dive,
Savour marmalade sandwiches, buttercup tea we revive,
The lucky fox ensures I'm home for tea,
He's my imaginary friend, dear to me.

# Empowerment

In a world woven with wonder and woe,
Laapataa Ladies let their luminous light show.
Sisters in spirit, they stand side by side,
Braving the battles, with bravery as their guide.

Their laughter, a lullaby to the lonely heart,
A beacon of bliss, a beautiful art.
Empowerment echoes in each earnest endeavour,
A chorus of courage, ceasing never.

Together they tread through trials and tears,
Sowing seeds of solidarity, silencing fears.
With whispers of wisdom like windswept waves,
Laapataa Ladies lead the way, bold and brave.

Hand in hand, they hold hope's helm,
Navigating life's realm with a resilient realm.
A sisterhood of souls so splendidly spun,
Under the universe's vast, vibrant sun

# The Path, The Verity, The Vital Spark

In the silence of prayer, where whispers ascend
A voice echoes softly, a guide to befriending.
"I am the way," it begins with a call,
A path through the wilderness, a rise after fall.

"The truth," it proclaims, in the darkness it shines,
A beacon of certainty, in uncertain times.
It speaks of a promise, a foundation so rife,
With the essence of trust, cutting doubt like a knife.

"The life," it breathes, a pulse within the soul,
A river of grace, making broken hearts whole.
It offers a journey, not just to survive,
But to thrive in love, eternally alive.

No roads lead astray, no lies to deceive,
For the way is clear, if we truly believe.
The truth is a lighthouse, the life is a flame,
In the name of the Father, through the Son, we reclaim.

# My life

I was born one day out of the blue
In the city of Wales, love was true.
Mum and Dad help my hand
I felt blessed to be born in a dragon land.

I was happy at school, I did my due,
My brother came along blond and true.
I went off to train to see the bright lights,
As a radiographer, I became, the world was bright.

My husband I met on a train filled with laughter,
In 1984 it became happy ever after.
Two happy children born of love,
And a nice big house with a blue sky above.

I have always loved writing, that's how it goes,
Knitting and cross stitching all in straight rows.
The time of my work has come to an end,
A wedding this week to join families and friends.

In the hills of my life, under skies of blue,
Our family is complete that much is true,
Two grandchildren go hand in hand,
In the place of my birth an enchanted land.

## Have you got time to stay a while?

Bodies crash, watching the sun go down,
My heart, feeling that old familiar sound,
Worlds apart, do you feel something too?
My soul is lit, no words can construe.

Do you have time to stay for a while?
Let's forget about the world, just you and I,
Underneath the stars, we'll let our worries fly,
Do you have time to stay for a while?

The music is new, but our hearts are old,
Lost in the melody, worth more than gold,
We can share a drink, dance through the night,
Up close and personal, everything feels right.

Oozing life our souls collide,
Words from your eyes, I can't help but feel alive,
So let's make this moment last,
This matters, dance, let go of the past.

Your perfumed breath, a perfect blend,
Holding you, my broken heart on the mend.
Embryonic love, do you feel it too?
Have you got time to stay a while, and love me true?

# Piano

I hear the soothing notes as you play
I see the colours as we swing and sway
I know you are sad, me too, I can tell
I feel your pain and bear this haunting hell.

We lost a child she was taken away
I hope she can forgive us someday
We tried so hard to get her back
We have music though it is black.

# Peking

Love snaps shut like a rusty trap,
Teeth honed on the bones of lost chaps.
Love howls relentlessly, through crumbling sleep,
Seeking remnants of humanity on which to leap.

Love renders steel and concrete portals,
Scraping hieroglyphs of doom into the immortal.
Once proud structures yield to serenity,
Their defiance was silenced by relentless captivity.

They roll together, a fiery ring,
A symphony of malevolence in Peking.
Their love binds them—a pact of the mind,
As they burrow into the heart of our kind.

Desperation drives us to barricade our love,
Wood against claw, metal against those from above.
We huddle in candlelit corners, whispering prayers,
As the love test our defences, our safe lairs.

Thus we stand together, prepared to see the stars,
To reconstruct, to recollect, to re-envision from afar.
Within this post-apocalyptic court, we discover, my dear,
And our love says, "We are still here."

# Tears fall

Tears fall and sorrows suck.
The world is out to get you.
You want to live happily ever after,
But your life is full of fear and longing.
You wonder when will it end.

You want beauty,
You want peace,
But all you see is pain.
Drain your life of the ocean and wonder.
You want the world to end.

Goodbye, peace,
Goodbye beauty,
And good riddance to struggles.
Drain your life of the ocean and wonder.
Your life doesn't have to end.

Sing with beauty,
Dance with peace,
And put a curse on the pain.
Your life is horrible,
But get out and live happily ever after.

You want the greatest thing
The clear sight, no crystal tears.
You've got it all, you've got it sized.
If you are confused check are you a mole?
Carry a vision to help be strong.

# Love and Hope

Today, a whole family said their final goodnight,
To this world, they cherished with all their might.
They were passengers in a car that met a crash,
And a motorbike lost two in this tragic dash.

As they ascend with God's grace on high,
We pray for their family and the space they can't deny.
The sorrow surpasses the tears that flowed,
May they be cared for in His abode.

The anguish and tears pour down like rain,
These innocent souls, from life, were untimely lain.
The sun will ascend, and the moon will wane,
Yet the sorrow lingers for those in God's domain.

For them all, I pray, and for you too,
Tears alone can't aid but hope and love see us through.
Cherish each moment as a divine fight,
Love those around you, and cherish our light.

We adapt to living with loss and ache,
Through summer's warmth and autumn's break.
In every droplet of rain and tear that falls,
May He navigate you through life's calls.

# Ode to the Bard of Avon

Oh, Shakespeare, the Bard of boundless fame,
Thy quill hath etched an immortal name.
In every line, a world's portrayed,
Where kings and jesters all have played.

Thou art the scribe of the human soul,
Whose plays unfold like scrolls unroll.
With words so rich, thou dost compose,
A tapestry that ever grows.

From Verona's streets to Danish gloom,
Thy tales outlive the tides of doom.
In sonnets sweet, love's essence caught,
Each verse is a treasure, finely wrought.

Forsooth, thy wit and wisdom shine,
In every metaphor and line.
The Globe still echoes with thy voice,
As generations still rejoice.

So here's to thee, oh timeless seer,
Whose legacy we hold so dear.
For in our hearts, thy verses chime,
Defying death, outlasting time.

# Patrick

Patrick lives in the Blue Sea,
He is as sweet as sweet can be.
Not too good at the math,
He enjoys a good bubble bath.

Patrick is a little bit overweight,
Wears green trunks on a first date.
He is SpongeBob's best friend,
But drives him around the seaweed bend.

The Bikini bottom is where they drive.
Under a ragged rock is his hive.
He has a big beating heart,
But not that star-shaped smart.

Patrick has his gameshow,
Letting us meet his family below.
Squidina, Mum and Dad and Grandpat,
He likes to talk, he loves to chat.

It must be great to live his life
No mortgage or nagging wife.
To live happily beneath the sea
Happy ever after, how it is meant to be.

# Psalm of Hope for the Captives

In captivity's shadowed halls,
Where sorrow dwells and heartache calls,
We raise our voices, O Divine,
For comfort and for freedom's sign.

O Captive seized against your wish,
Be assured you're not dismissed.
Even if nations waver and stall,
Our supplications like incense fall.

A candle of hope in the gloom flickers slightly,
Leading the way to the dawn of right.
O Captive, endure, endure,
As deliverance softly murmurs sure.

In the hush of confinement's grip,
Let bravery like desert blooms slip.
Families, unwavering, tired of the fight,
Join hands beyond the divide's blight.

A candle of hope in the gloom flickers slightly,
Leading the way to the dawn of right.
O Captive, endure, endure,
As deliverance softly murmurs sure.

Guardians celestial in realms unseen,
Brush despair with wings serene.

Bearing love's missives, they soar,
Over spiked wire and barred door.

A candle of hope in the gloom flickers slight,
Leading the way to the dawn of right.
O Captive, endure, endure,
As deliverance softly murmurs sure.

As chains release their bitter clasp,
And daylight's kiss prompts you to gasp,
Step forth into the day anew,
Wrapped in freedom's loving hue.

# Character cards

Lawful Good: William Wordsworth

In nature's laws, he found his faithful guide,
With every step, a landscape is glorified.
A poet's heart, with lawful goodness filled,
In tranquil dales, his verses sweetly spilled.

Neutral Good: Emily Dickinson

A recluse soul, with a neutral stance, but kind,
Her words were a balm to every troubled mind.
In dashes and hymns, her thoughts took flight,
A beacon shining in the quiet night.

Chaotic Good: Oscar Wilde

With wit as sharp as any thorned rose,
His chaotic charm, through every sentence, flows.
For art's own sake, he played the dandy part,
Good at the core, with an unruly heart.

Lawful Neutral: Geoffrey Chaucer

With ordered tales, a pilgrimage he penned,
A tapestry where many journeys blend.
In Middle English verse, he found his tune,
The lawful scribe beneath the harvest moon.

True Neutral: T.S. Eliot

In measured lines, the world's complexities,
He captured life's inherent dualities.
A neutral gaze upon the human plight,
In verses dense as foggy London night.

Chaotic Neutral: Hunter S. Thompson

In gonzo tales of fear and loathing, found,
A voice that echoed with a chaotic sound.
No rules could bind his wild, unbridled zest,
A neutral rogue who put the world to the test.

Lawful Evil: Niccolo Machiavelli

With laws of power, he advised the throne,
In politics, his cunning mind is well-known.
A prince's guide, with lawful evil's taint,
His verses veiled his portrait like a saint.

Neutral Evil: Marquis de Sade

In darkest ink, his quill would dance and taunt,
A neutral evil, his forbidden want.
In pleasure's pain, his narratives would weave,
A shadow lurking in the velvet eve.

Chaotic Evil: Edgar Allan Poe

In Raven's call and the Tell-tale Heart,
A chaotic evil in his art did start.
With madness tinged, his tales of dark despair,
A genius mind, disturbed beyond compare.

# 1977

Feathers of colour, vibrant and free,
Reflect the spirit's deep decree.
With every beat, the heart does sing,
A timeless song, an endless spring.

Beyond the skirt, beyond the face,
Lies the true essence, a gentle grace.
In every smile, in every tear,
The heart's true voice is so pure and clear.

Soar above, with wings unseen,
In realms where the heart is queen.
For, in the end, it's love's embrace,
That carries us with gentle grace.

Through trials faced and battles fought,
It's graciousness that can't be bought.
A silent strength, a quiet power,
That blooms within, a radiant flower.

In the quiet of the night, where shadows dance,
A whisper of grace, a fleeting glance.
For in the heart, where stories engage,
Lies the true beauty, ageless sage.

# Thomas Carney

In verses penned with faith's ink,
Thomas Carney made us think.
His words, a tapestry of grace,
Wove through the fabric of our space.

An inspiring Thomas yet a guide,
To question, seek, and not to hide.
His poems, like a lighthouse beam,
Illuminated the unseen dream.

Through metaphors and rhythmic flow,
He shared a truth we all could know.
A mirror to our soul's own plight,
His verses brought our hearts to light.

In memory of a poet true,
Whose lines were heartfelt, deep, and new.
Thomas Carney's words remain,
A testament to life's refrain.

So let us read, reflect, and pause,
To honour him and his life's cause.
For in his poetry, we find,
A legacy of the enduring kind.

# Eliora

Eliora was not just a figure among the poppies; she was their guardian, their whisperer.
With a gentle sway of her hand, the flowers swayed, releasing tiny sparks of light, like fireflies at dusk.

Her laughter was the melody that summoned the butterflies, each wingbeat a note in her symphony of joy.
The square on her back, a patchwork of dreams, fluttered with the magic of unseen worlds, a tapestry of tales spun from stardust and moonbeams.

Eliora, the light-bringer, danced in the embrace of the wind, her steps light, her spirit untamed. In her eyes, if one could see them, lay the shimmer of faraway galaxies, a reflection of the whimsical soul that dwelled within.

# Comfort

Comfort for the brave,
A blanket against the cold,
Angels' arms enfold,
Holding you tightly.
You've given everything,
Now drained, weary, and faint,
Comfort arises,
In a divine radiance.
You stand not alone,
Help is within reach.
Comfort marches forth into
A room cradling your heart,
Filled with warmth
And love from above.